MW01172469

SELFCATION:

Unlock Your Potential through Self Discovery

Dr. Elnaz Zahed

Imprint: Independently Published

ISBN: 9798869766199
Imprint: Independently published

ASIN: B0CNW1K2N5
ASIN: B0CTF689TB

Cover design by: Mariane Khater

Printed in the United States of America

Selfcation

Preface

Dear You,

I'm excited to share with you a unique perspective in the "Selfcation" book. "Selfcation" book distinguishes itself by seamlessly integrating the wisdom derived from scholarly research with the authenticity that comes from lived experiences.

As a psychotherapist, my commitment to providing you with valuable insights is underpinned by a robust academic background. The content you'll find within these thoughtfully crafted pages isn't merely anecdotal; it's a synthesis of evidence-based practices, psychological theories, and the latest scientific findings. I firmly believe that the intersection of academic knowledge and real-world application is where transformative potential lies.

Thank you for embarking on this intellectually stimulating and personally enriching journey with me.

Warm regards,

Dr. Elnaz Zahed

Psychotherapist

List of Contents

Before you heal people, ask them if they're willing to give up the things that make them sick.

Hippocrates

1. Introduction:

Welcome to "Selfcation: Unlocking Your Potential through Self Discovery", a guidebook designed to inspire and empower you on a transformative voyage of self-discovery. This book is your invitation to embark on a unique "Selfcation", a deliberate and mindful journey inward, where you'll explore the uncharted territories of your thoughts, feelings, and aspirations.

In the pages that follow, we'll navigate the terrain of self-discovery, offering insights, exercises, and reflections that encourage you to ponder, reflect, and reconnect with the person you are at your core. Whether you're seeking a deeper understanding of your passions, purpose, or simply a moment of tranquility in your busy life, "Selfcation" is your compass for navigating the path to self-awareness and self-improvement.

Join me on this introspective adventure, where each chapter unveils a new facet of yourself, and every page turns into an opportunity for growth. Let's embark on this journey together, unlocking the mysteries within and cultivating a richer, more authentic version of yourself. The path to self-discovery awaits, are you ready to embark on the ultimate "Selfcation"?

Welcome to the "Selfcation" Journey

In a world brimming with distractions and external influences, it's easy to lose sight of the most important person in your life: yourself. "Selfcation" is an invitation to start off a journey that places you at the center of your narrative. It's a journey of self-discovery, personal growth, and empowerment, where you hold the pen and write your story.

Are you ready to take the driver's seat in your life? To chart a course that aligns with your values, dreams, and aspirations? If so, you're in the right place.

In these pages, we'll explore the empowering concept of the "Selfcation". This means embracing a mindset and lifestyle where your needs, desires, and authentic self, take precedence. It is about understanding that personal growth, fulfillment, and success begin from within you and that your journey is uniquely yours.

Self-acceptance is a key milestone on the path of the "Selfcation". It involves embracing both the light and shadow within you, acknowledging imperfections, and celebrating the uniqueness that sets you apart. This acceptance is not a destination but a continuous process of learning, growing, and evolving.

Change and transformation will be constant companions on your "Selfcation" journey. You'll come to embrace these as opportunities for growth and self-reinvention.

By the time you reach the final page, you'll have the tools and insights to continue this self-directed journey, weaving the principles of "Selfcation" into every aspect of your life.

So, if you're ready to put yourself at the forefront, explore your true potential, and navigate your life in a way that resonates with your innermost desires, let's begin this transformative journey together. Your story begins here, with the "Selfcation" mindset leading the way.

Take a notebook and register your responses to the exercises and assignments throughout the book. You revisit the assignments to complete them more thoroughly. By the end of this book, you have your "Selfcation" roadmap for yourself that can guide you in your life journey. All the concepts you learn in this book are interconnected, and you gradually complete them step by step. By the end of this book, you will have a manual for yourself, which can continue to be developed beyond these pages because you have learned how to do it.

So, welcome to the "Selfcation" journey, a transformative expedition where the destination is not a fixed point on the horizon but a continuous unfolding of your truest self. May this journey be filled with self-discovery, acceptance, and profound realisation.

Seize the moment and invest in yourself through your "Selfcation" journey.

Welcome to the adventure of self-discovery and personal growth. Welcome to the "Selfcation" journey.

What Does "Selfcation" Mean?

In psychology and philosophy, the "self" refers to the individual as a distinct, unified entity with a unique identity. It encompasses a person's thoughts, feelings, perceptions, and experiences. 'Cation' refers to a positively charged ion. It is formed when an atom or a group of atoms loses one or more electrons. The loss of electrons results in an excess of positive charge, leading to the formation of a cation. Having said the meaning of different parts of "Selfcation" you can guess what "Selfcation" tries to convey.

Please write down your thoughts on the meaning of "Selfcation" and soon you read my explanation.

The path of "Selfcation" is a dynamic process, a continuous unraveling of the unique tapestry that makes you who you are. It is a conscious commitment to peeling away the masks you wear, shedding societal expectations, and embracing the essence of your true self. This journey requires courage, vulnerability, and a willingness to confront the various facets of your identity. Note that as you peel away layers, removing and deducting from yourself, it's akin to the process of the 'Cation' losing one or more electrons. This loss results in an increase in positive charge. By constantly and intentionally stripping away layers you've added to yourself, you move closer to your true self. The journey of "Selfcation" is not about adding, it's about reducing and peeling off to reach your true and authentic self.

In the realm of "Selfcation", introspection becomes your compass, guiding you through the labyrinth of your emotions, experiences, and aspirations. It is a reflective practice that encourages you to question, explore, and understand the stories you tell yourself about who you are and who you ought to be. Through introspection, you gain insights into your values, passions, and the core principles that shape your worldview.

As you navigate this expedition, be prepared to challenge preconceived notions, both internal and external, societal expectations, cultural influences, and personal biases may have woven intricate threads into the fabric of your identity. "Selfcation" prompts you to examine these threads, discerning between those that align with your authentic self and those that may have been woven by external pressures.

5

Vulnerability becomes a powerful ally on this journey. It is through vulnerability that you unearth the raw, unfiltered aspects of your being. Embracing vulnerability allows you to connect with your emotions, acknowledge your fears, and confront the parts of yourself you may have kept hidden. It is in these vulnerable moments that authenticity finds its truest expression.

When I mention "Selfcation", it doesn't mean to be selfish. I'm emphasising the distinction between "Selfcation" and Selfishness. It's crucial to recognise and prioritise your needs, values, and well-being without neglecting the needs and concerns of others. Here's a breakdown of the "Selfcation" and Selfishness to shed light on the difference between these two concepts:

❖ **Selfcation:**

Self-awareness: Understanding your emotions, motivations, strengths, vulnerability, and weaknesses is a fundamental aspect of the "Selfcation". It involves introspection and a deep exploration of your identity.

Personal growth: Prioritising your personal development and growth is a positive aspect of "Selfcation". This can involve setting and pursuing goals, acquiring new skills, and embracing opportunities for learning and enrichment.

Setting boundaries: "Selfcation" includes recognising your limits and setting boundaries. This is not about shutting others out but about maintaining a healthy balance in your relationships and commitments.

❖ **Selfishness:**

Lack of consideration: Selfishness often involves a disregard for the needs and feelings of others. It manifests as a self-centered approach where personal desires take precedence over the well-being of those around you.

Harm to others: Selfish behaviour may lead to negative consequences for others. This can strain relationships and create an environment of mistrust and conflict.

Inability to compromise: A selfish person may be unwilling to compromise or collaborate, making it challenging to build healthy and mutually beneficial relationships.

More insight about the "Selfcation" lies in balancing it with consideration for others:

Healthy relationships: "Selfcation" doesn't mean disregarding the needs of others. In fact, a strong sense of self-awareness can contribute to healthier relationships by fostering open communication and mutual understanding.

Empathy and compassion: Understanding your needs can enhance your ability to empathise with others. A balanced approach involves considering the perspectives and feelings of those around you.

Contributing to the community: A well-rounded you, who is self-aware and on the path of "Selfcation", can contribute positively to your community and society. This contribution is often rooted in a sense of purpose and fulfillment derived from understanding your values and making a meaningful impact.

"Selfcation" is a term that signifies the process of recognising, validating, and affirming your authentic self. It involves a deep exploration and understanding of your identity, values, beliefs, and personal characteristics. The concept suggests a conscious and intentional journey towards living in alignment with your genuine nature, free from external influences or societal expectations.

The term "Selfcation" encapsulates the idea that each individual has a unique and authentic essence that goes beyond external appearances or societal norms. It implies a commitment to self-discovery, self-awareness, and self-acceptance, a journey where you seek to understand and embrace your true identity, regardless of external pressures or influences.

Throughout this book, you'll learn how to cultivate a growth mindset in your "Selfcation" journey that propels you toward your goals. We'll discuss setting and pursuing meaningful objectives, nurturing your relationships, prioritising self-care and wellness, and achieving financial and career empowerment.

All in all, "Selfcation" is about understanding and fulfilling your needs in a healthy and constructive manner. It involves personal growth, setting boundaries, and maintaining a sense of identity. However, it should not be confused with selfishness, which involves a lack of consideration for others. "Selfcation" means accepting yourself with all your flaws, weaknesses, and vulnerabilities, then try to change them to become the truest self and the best version of yourself. The concept of 'Accept first and then change' is derived from Dialectical Behaviour Therapy (DBT), which we will discuss later in this book.

Self-understanding rather than self-condemnation is the way to inner peace and mature conscience.

Joshua L. Liebman

2. Self-Discovery and Awareness

Self-exploration and personal introspection are integral aspects of personal development and growth. They involve gaining insight into your identity, values, beliefs, strengths, weaknesses, and emotions. This process is often ongoing and can lead to a deeper understanding of yourself and a more authentic and fulfilling life that leads you to "Selfcation". To start off here are the key practices of self-discovery and awareness. It is important to have a clear picture of your current status by doing these tasks. You revisit them throughout the book for potential changes. Bring your pen and notebook and start writing about the below tasks:

1. Reflection:

Taking time for introspection and reflection is crucial for self-discovery. This involves examining your thoughts, feelings, and actions, and considering how they align with your values and goals.

Reflect on your current status, by what you've learnt about "Selfcation", and what you expect to get from this book.

2. Mindfulness:

Practicing mindfulness involves being fully present in the moment without judgement. Mindfulness techniques, such as meditation and deep breathing, can help increasing self-awareness by focusing attention on the present. Adhering to "Here and Now" is an important factor in mindfulness.

The mindfulness that we talk about in this book is backed up by Dialectical Behaviour Therapy (DBT). DBT is a psychotherapy developed by Marsha Linehan. It combines Cognitive Behavioural Therapy (CBT) techniques with mindfulness and Eastern philosophy. DBT focuses on balancing acceptance and change, teaching skills in mindfulness, interpersonal effectiveness, emotion regulation, and distress tolerance. It's effective for various mental health conditions, and can be implemented in both individual and group therapy sessions. The structured approach helps individuals manage emotions, improve relationships, and cope with crises. I don't want to make this book like a university book. This book is backed by science while remaining practical, offering benefits that you can apply in your daily life.

Before going to the next task, practice mindfulness, i.e., pay attention to here and now and collect yourself to be fully present in the here and now.

3. Values and Beliefs:

Understanding your core values and beliefs is essential for self-discovery. These principles guide your decisions and actions, shaping your identity and the way you interact with the world.

Take a deep breath, ponder, and write down your values and beliefs related to self-discovery and awareness now.

4. Strengths and Weaknesses:

Identifying your strengths and weaknesses enables you to leverage your positive attributes and work on areas that may need improvement. This self-awareness can be valuable in personal and professional contexts in the "Selfcation" journey. It helps you to gain good knowledge about yourself.

Be honest with yourself. Write down your strengths and weaknesses concerning your values and beliefs. What are the facilitators in your journey of "Selfcation," and what are the hindrances and areas for improvement?

5. Emotional Intelligence:

Recognising and understanding your emotions, as well as the emotions of others, contributes to emotional intelligence. This skill enhances your ability to navigate social interactions, manage stress, and make informed decisions.

Also, it can be a good take-in for calculated risks that we will discuss later. Just to give you an idea, calculated risks usually are manageable risks that you plan and calculate their consequences.

Consider situations where your emotional intelligence can come to the forefront and provide valuable assistance.

6. Life Experiences:

Life experiences, both positive and negative, play a significant role in self-discovery. Challenges and successes offer opportunities for learning and growth, shaping your self-perception and resilience. Life experiences provide valuable opportunities for exposure to diversity, as well as challenges and adversity.

Exposure to diversity provides opportunities to interact with people from different backgrounds and exposes you to diverse perspectives, beliefs, and values. This exposure can challenge your preconceptions, broaden your understanding, and lead to self-discovery as you reflect on your beliefs concerning others.

Challenges and adversity offer the ground for facing challenges and overcoming adversity often brings out inner strengths and resilience that you may not have been aware of. These experiences can reveal your capacity for problem-solving, coping mechanisms, personal growth, and contributing significantly to self-awareness.

Try to remember a few such experiences and write down the lessons you've learnt.

7.   Goals and Aspirations:

Clearly defining your goals and aspirations helps you understand what is truly important to you. This clarity guides your actions and decisions, creating a sense of purpose and direction. Your goals and aspirations work like a compass to keep you on the track.

Express your goals and aspirations with words. Make them visible by describing them through words.

8.   Continuous Learning:

Embracing a mindset of continuous learning nurtures personal development. This can involve exploring new interests, acquiring new skills, or challenging existing beliefs, leading to a more enriched and evolving sense of self throughout the "Selfcation" journey. You'll obtain more knowledge about the mindset later in this book.

Think about the last time you learn something. Was it intentional learning?

Also, ponder whether there are any opportunities for learning in your current situation.

9.   Feedback:

Seeking and receiving feedback from others can offer valuable perspectives on your strengths and areas for improvement. Constructive feedback is a valuable tool for self-awareness. Keep in mind that reflection works in almost the same way and both can assist you in your self-development journey of the "Selfcation". Reflection is the feedback you receive from yourself. Both self-reflection and feedback from others are important components that we emphasise on knowledge about yourself throughout your "Selfcation" journey.

Ask your friends, colleagues, or mentor to give you feedback to help you on your personal development journey of the "Selfcation". If you receive constructive feedback, don't feel frustrated; consider it as a compass guiding you toward your goals.

10. Acceptance:

Acceptance of yourself, including both strengths and imperfections, is a key aspect of self-discovery. Consider yourself as a whole, not bits and pieces. Embracing who you are without judgement allows for genuine personal growth. It helps you to see your true self and take your true self back from yourself. Regain your true self. In your life step by step, you take distance from yourself to indulge in society and fulfill outside expectations. Now is the time to visit yourself to see your true self in your "Selfcation" journey.

Consider whether there are things you do due to external pressure and think about what you can do to rectify them.

Self-discovery is a lifelong process, and you may engage in various practices and experiences to deepen your understanding of yourself. It is a process that evolves over time and can lead to greater self-acceptance, resilience, and the ability to live authentically that are required in your "Selfcation" journey.

Pour yourself a cup of tea or coffee and welcome yourself to the adventurous world of "Selfcation". Review your notes on the tasks and then, turn the page to explore your authentic self.

Chapter 1

Exploring Your Authentic Self

In this foundational chapter, we continue the exciting concept of self-exploration. You'll discover the significance of uncovering your authentic self, the person you are when you strip away societal expectations and external influences. Through thought-provoking exercises and introspective questions, you'll start to peel back the layers to reveal your true essence. This chapter will encourage you to embrace your uniqueness and understand that authenticity is the key to a fulfilling life. You explore your uniqueness in the process of the "Selfcation".

Exploring your authentic self involves engaging in activities that encourage self-reflection, introspection, and a deeper understanding of your values, passions, and true identity. Here are some exercises to help you in this lifelong exploration. Bring your notebook and pen and start:

1. Journaling:

Regularly write in a journal about your thoughts, feelings, and experiences. Reflect on your day, your reactions to various situations, and your long-term goals. Journaling can provide insights into patterns of behaviour and emotions.

Moreover, journaling is a tangible measure that you can revisit to evaluate your progress.

You can start journalling like a diary till you get the hang of journalling. Also, you can begin by incorporating thoughts about your current understanding of this book's content or by sharing your plans and objectives for what you hope to achieve by the end of this book. You can start by adding something related to your reading so far or about the plans you have in your mind to achieve by the end of this book.

2. Values Clarification:

Refer to the list you wrote in the previous section, edit it if needed, and adding your core values and priorities them if you didn't do it before, i.e., identify the values that are most important to you. Consider how these values align with your daily actions and life choices. Adjustments may be needed to be more in line with your authentic self.

Read your list loud for yourself. You can record your voice and listen to it again and register your thoughts and feelings.

3. Strengths and Weaknesses Assessment:

Read the list you wrote in the previous section and make an inventory of your strengths and weaknesses. Identify what activities or situations make you feel most alive and fulfilled. Recognise areas where you would like to improve. This exercise helps you leverage your strengths and work on personal development in your "Selfcation" journey.

Spend some additional time on this list, aiming to make it as comprehensive as possible. Review the list and reflect on whether you would like to have a friend with the same qualities as yourself. If the answer is yes, kudos to you. If the answer is no, consider identifying the characteristics you want to change in this hypothetical friend.

Introspection is suggested for preparing this list.

4. Mindfulness Meditation:

Practice mindfulness meditation to cultivate present-moment awareness. This can help you connect with your authentic self by allowing you to observe your thoughts without distraction and judgement and fostering a deeper understanding of your inner world.

Put your notebook aside. Close your eyes and mindfully be present and pay attention to the here and now. Hear yourself and try to see yourself while your eyes are closed.

5. Letter to Your Younger Self:

Write a letter to your younger self, offering advice, encouragement, and insights gained from your current perspective. This exercise can provide clarity on the lessons you've learnt and the values that have shaped you.

Don't forget to be thankful to yourself.

You can begin your letter by Dear Younger Me.

6. Letter to Your Older Self:

Write a letter to your older self to express your gratitude for accompanying yourself all through the life span and life's ups and downs. Tell yourself how proud you are of yourself. Remind your achievements, challenges, and lessons you learnt from them.

You can start off your letter by Dear Future Me. Keep the letter in hand because we revisit it soon.

7. Bucket List Creation:

Create a bucket list of things you want to experience, achieve, or learn in your lifetime. This exercise helps uncover your passions and desires, providing a roadmap for a life that lines up with your authentic self. Clear your mind from limitations and write a list to help you discover your inner self, passion, and aspiration.

It is a good idea to calm down more by practicing mindful meditation prior to write this list.

8. Disconnecting from External Influences:

Take a break from external influences such as social media, news, and other distractions. Spend time alone to reflect on your thoughts and feelings without external pressures. This can help you reconnect with your inner self. Observe your feelings when you are disconnected from social media.

Check whether you experience anxiety or feel an urge to connect with others on social media.

Set a deadline for yourself, e.g. in the next one hour or one day or whatsoever, you'll be disconnected from social media.

9. Creative Expression:

Engage in a form of creative expression, whether it's writing, drawing, painting, playing a musical instrument, etc. Creative activities can provide a channel for expressing your authentic self in a way that may be challenging through daily activities and daily life.

Unleash your inner self by creative expression in your "Selfcation" journey.

You can draw something simple in your notebook such as a flower or a house like childhood drawings and make a story for it. Reflect on the story. Try to check whether you can find a connection between the story and your authentic self.

10. Life Timeline:

Create a timeline of your life, noting significant events, achievements, and challenges. Reflect on how these experiences have shaped you. This exercise can reveal patterns and themes that contribute to your authentic self. In a more academic term, it is a kind of 'Autoethnography' that can reveal turning points in your life. If you are curious enough, look for autoethnography to get more information that assists in this exercise.

Now, think about turning points in your life and write them down.

Can you find any trends among them, e.g., experiencing repeated success or unsuccess?

11. Ask for Feedback:

Seek feedback from close friends, family, or mentors about how they perceive you. Others may provide insights into your strengths and qualities that you might not see in yourself.

Also, your self-reflection works in the same manner we talked about here.

You can call someone to ask for feedback now and if it is not possible, give such feedback through self-reflection.

Remember that exploring your authentic self is an ongoing process. Be patient and compassionate with yourself as you engage in these exercises, and allow the insights gained to guide your journey toward a more authentic and fulfilling life in your "Selfcation" journey.

In the coming chapter, the power of self-awareness will be discussed.

Chapter 2

The Power of Self-Awareness

S elf-awareness is the cornerstone of personal growth. In this chapter, we'll dive deep into the concept of self-awareness and its transformative potential. You'll explore how knowing yourself, your strengths, weaknesses, triggers, and values, can lead to better decision-making, improved relationships, and a more meaningful life. You find practical strategies and self-assessment tools that you can apply to enhance your self-awareness, empowering yourself to make conscious choices that align with your true self in the "Selfcation" journey.

The power of self-awareness lies in its ability to profoundly impact various aspects of your life, including personal development, relationships, decision-making, and overall well-being. We are going through some key aspects that highlight the significance of self-awareness in your "Selfcation".

Understanding Emotions: Self-awareness involves recognising and understanding your emotions. The emotional intelligence, that we talked about, is crucial for managing and expressing feelings appropriately, both for yourself and in interpersonal relationships.

Both the British Psychological Society (BPS) and the American Psychology Association (APA) believe emotions are complex reaction patterns, involving experiential, behavioural, and physiological elements. Emotions are how individuals deal with matters or situations they find personally significant.

Apply this definition to yourself, and you can gain better insight and resonate with your emotions in an informed manner.

Improved Decision-Making: A heightened sense of self-awareness allows you to make decisions that align with your values, goals, and long-term objectives. Also, it echoes your strengths and weaknesses in the process of making decisions to protect yourself. It helps in avoiding impulsive choices and ensures a more intentional and thoughtful decision-making process.

Enhanced Interpersonal Relationships: Being aware of your strengths, weaknesses, and emotional triggers brings up healthier relationships. Self-aware individuals can communicate more effectively, empathise with others, and navigate conflicts with greater understanding.

Personal Development and Growth: Self-awareness is the foundation of personal development. It enables you to identify areas for improvement, set realistic goals, and actively work towards becoming the best version of yourself. The continuous process of self-reflection contributes to ongoing growth.

Authenticity and Identity: Self-awareness allows you to connect with your authentic self. It involves acknowledging your values, beliefs, passions, and aspirations leading to a more genuine and prosperous life that is aligned with your authentic identity. Embracing your authentic self involves being true to your thoughts, feelings, and desires, even if they differ from external norms or pressures.

Increased Empathy: A strong sense of self-awareness is often accompanied with increased empathy towards yourself and others. When you understand your emotions and experiences, you are better equipped to relate to and understand the perspectives of those around you. Also, you become kinder to yourself. Moreover, you withhold judgement, and try to understand yourself and others better. Accordingly, you become more considerate.

Effective Communication: Self-aware you tend to communicate more clearly and authentically. You are conscious of your communication style, including verbal and non-verbal clues, leading to more effective and meaningful interactions with yourself and others. In addition, less misunderstanding may happen in your relationships.

Resilience in the Face of Challenges: Self-awareness contributes to resilience. You understand your strengths and weaknesses and can trace challenges with a more balanced perspective. You are better equipped to learn from setbacks and adapt to changing circumstances without feeling frustrated and helpless.

Resilience doesn't mean you don't feel anything. It refers to the ability to move through and grow from difficult times. It's a skill you develop over time from the lessons and experiences you absorb as you grow up and face challenges.

Helplessness can be learnt, so be alert that it doesn't happen. You can refer to learnt helplessness by Seligman if you want to know more.

Alignment with Life Purpose: Basically, the power of self-awareness lies in its transformative ability to positively influence various facets of life. It empowers you to navigate challenges, build meaningful connections, and pursue a path of personal growth and authenticity.

Achieving a deep level of self-awareness often involves exploring your passions and values. This exploration helps you line up your actions and life choices with a sense of purpose, leading to a more meaningful and accomplished life. Cultivating self-awareness is an ongoing journey that can lead to a more conscious and intentional way of living in the "Selfcation".

Now, take a deep breath, review what you have read and learnt so far, and then read the letter to your future self. Writing a letter to your future self, as we mentioned before, can be a powerful and reflective exercise. It allows you to set intentions, express your current aspirations, create a snapshot of your present self, and determine the trajectory for your future self.

Keep the letter in hand and reflect on it after each chapter that you read. This letter can add value to your self-awareness in your "Selfcation" journey.

Here are some suggestions on what to include in a letter to your older self to assist you in the self-awareness:

1. Current State of Mind:

Begin by describing your current state of mind and emotions. What are your feelings right now? Acknowledge any challenges or triumphs you are experiencing.

2. Goals and Aspirations:

Outline your current goals and aspirations. What do you hope to achieve in the coming months or years? Again, be specific about both personal and professional goals.

3. Values and Principles:

Reflect on your core values and principles. Are there specific values you want to bring into realisation in your future self? Consider how these values line up with your goals and choices. Also, determine what they can add to your life.

They should be valuable enough to keep you on the track at the time of storm and turmoil.

4. Lessons Learnt:

Share insights and lessons you've learnt from recent experiences. Reflect on how these lessons have shaped your perspective, influenced your decisions, and what their takeaways are for the future.

5. Gratitude:

Express gratitude for different aspects of your life. What are you thankful for at this moment? Recognise the people, opportunities, and experiences that infuse happiness and satisfaction.

In addition, be thankful for and recognise the experiences that did not bring happy moments with them. In long run, they may add valuable insights to your life.

6. Current Interests and Passions:

Describe your current interests and passions. What activities or hobbies are bringing you joy and satisfaction? Consider how you can continue to incorporate these into your future life.

7. Challenges and Coping Strategies:

If you are facing challenges, discuss them openly. What strategies are you employing to overcome obstacles? This section can serve as a reminder of your resilience and problem-solving abilities and the coping strategies you are applying now, can be the bedrock of your future coping strategies. You find more information about the coping strategies in chapter 15 Managing Stress and Finding Balance.

8. Personal Growth Aspirations:

Share your thoughts on personal growth. How do you envision evolving as an individual? What steps are you taking to help continuous self-improvement? What is your plan in this regard?

Consider traits that you want to change during the journey of your "Selfcation". You know which traits I mean. Let's call them the electrons to lose to become more positively charged.

9. Relationships:

Reflect on your current relationships. First, reflect on your relationship with yourself, i.e., the relationship between you with yourself. Try to resonate with your inner and authentic self as much as you can. Then, your relationship with others. How do these connections contribute to your life, and what role do you see them playing in your future?

10. Words of Encouragement:

Write encouraging words to your future self. Remind yourself of your strengths, capabilities, and the resilience you've demonstrated in the past. Offer words of support for the challenges that may lie ahead.

11. Closing Reflection:

Conclude the letter to your future self with a final reflection on your present self. What do you want your future self to remember about this moment in your life? Consider any commitments or promises you want to make to yourself.

You can add more to the letter to your future self step by step as you read this book and walk on the "Selfcation" path.

Remember after you finish this book, do the final touch-ups to the letter, seal it, and set a date in the future when you'll open and read this letter. This exercise not only provides a snapshot of your current self but also serves as a measure or a time capsule, allowing you to witness your growth and evolution over time and measure "Selfcation" in your life path.

In the coming chapter, you find suggestions to identify your passions and values.

Chapter 3

Identifying Your Passions and Values

Passions and values guide your life's journey. In this chapter, we explore the process of identifying what truly matters to you. We'll discuss the significance of aligning your actions and aspirations with your core values and passions. Through reflective exercises and real-life examples, you'll gain a clear understanding of what ignites your enthusiasm and fuels your purpose. By the end of this chapter, you'll be equipped to live a life that reflects your authentic self and resonates with your deepest values more than before.

Identifying your passions and values is a deeply personal and introspective process that echoes your uniqueness. Here are some practical exercises to help you discover and clarify your passions and values:

Identifying Passions:

1. Reflect on Childhood Interests:

Consider activities you were naturally drawn to during your childhood. Often, our early interests provide clues about our passions. Over time, our interests may be manipulated to serve the outside world and others more than ourselves. We need to discover our inner passion and what we are good at by peeling off layers of outside pressure and manipulation.

2. Explore Different Hobbies:

Engage in a variety of hobbies and activities. Pay attention to those that bring you excitement, a sense of fulfillment, and satisfaction. Your passion may lie in one of these pursuits. Be alert and conscious of your feelings while experiencing these hobbies. Unleash your inner self to experience different activities.

3. Journaling:

In chapter 1, Exploring Your Authentic Self, you practiced the journalling. You can add this and other journalling practices to it. Regularly journal about your experiences, feelings, and activities. Take note of moments when you feel most alive and enthusiastic. Patterns may emerge that point to your passions.

You may find trends in your experiences, feelings, and activities that may lead to the discovery of your passions.

4.   Ask Yourself What You Would Do If Nothing Hinders You:

If you didn't have to worry about limitations like financial constraints, what activities would you choose to spend your time on? The answer might reveal your true passions.

5.   Seek New Experiences:

Step out of your comfort zone and try new things. Attend events, workshops, or classes that interest you. Exposure to diverse experiences can help you discover what resonates with you.

By exposing yourself to new experiences, you may discover something about yourself that you were not aware of before.

6.   Pay Attention to Your Energy Level:

Notice how different activities affect your energy level. Your passions are likely to be activities that energise and motivate you rather than drain you.

Bear in mind that it is possible to be an expert in something you are scared of. Take a moment to observe your feelings, thoughts, and emotions. Pay attention to your energy level, whether it's high or low. In both cases, they may provide valuable hints. Listen to your inner self. Be quite to hear your inner self.

Identifying Values:

1.   Reflect on Core Beliefs:

Write down your beliefs and then prioritise them. Consider the principles that are most important to you. What do you believe in? Your values often align with your core beliefs.

2.   Identify Peak Moments:

Recall moments in your life when you felt truly fulfilled and satisfied. Analyse what made those moments special, as they may be connected to your values.

3.   Define Personal Success:

Reflect on what success means to you personally. The definition of success often reflects your values. What achievements are most meaningful to you?

4. Prioritise:

Make a list of your current priorities in life, e.g. work, family, etc. What you prioritise reflects your values. Reevaluate and adjust your priorities based on what truly matters to you.

5. Examine Role Models:

Identify individuals you admire and consider why you look up to them. The qualities you appreciate in others can indicate the values you hold.

6. Explore What Makes You Angry or Upset:

Sometimes, our strongest reactions are linked to our values. Reflect on situations or events that make you angry or upset, and consider what values are being challenged.

What can distort your logical thought process, actions, and behaviours?

Remember that discovering your passions and values is an ongoing process and they may change over time. Be patient with yourself, and assign time for self-reflection and exploration. Regularly revisit and refine your understanding of your passions and values as you grow and evolve. These are necessary for the "Selfcation" journey. Be reminded that all these concepts are intertwined and they are not isolated from each other.

In the next part the mindset and personal growth will be explained.

One day, in retrospect, the years of struggle will strike you as the most beautiful.

Sigmund Freud

3. Mindset and Personal Growth

The concept of mindset plays a crucial role in your personal development including the "Selfcation" journey. It influences how you perceive challenges, approach learning, how you know yourself, and navigate the journey of self-improvement. Two prominent mindsets are often recognised in the context of personal growth, i.e., the fixed mindset and the growth mindset. We are going to discuss them.

Fixed Mindset:

Individuals with a fixed mindset believe that their abilities, intelligence, and talents are fixed traits. They tend to avoid challenges, fear failure, may perceive the effort as fruitless, and view failure as a sign of inadequacy.

In a fixed mindset, challenges are seen as threats, and setbacks or failures are taken personally. The focus is often on proving oneself rather than embracing the opportunity for learning and growth.

Feedback that implies a lack of inherent talent or intelligence may be disregarded or seen as criticism rather than an opportunity for improvement.

Growth Mindset:

Individuals with a growth mindset, on the other hand, believe that their abilities and intelligence can be developed through dedication and hard work. They embrace challenges, see effort as the path to mastery, and view failures as opportunities to learn and improve.

In a growth mindset, challenges are viewed as opportunities to expand one's skills and knowledge. Setbacks are seen as a natural part of the learning process, and individuals are more resilient in the face of difficulties.

Feedback, even if critical, is seen as constructive and an avenue for improvement. Individuals with a growth mindset value the learning process over the appearance of competence.

As you can guess in the journey of "Selfcation" you need to nurture the growth mindset that opens up and paves the personal development pathway. In the coming section, the impact of the growth mindset and personal growth is explained to encourage you to adopt such a mindset.

Learning Orientation: A growth mindset assists a learning orientation where you actively seek out opportunities for learning and development. Challenges are seen as a chance to acquire new skills and knowledge.

Resilience in the Face of Setbacks: By adopting the growth mindset, you tend to be more resilient in the face of setbacks. You view failures as stepping stones to success and are more likely to persevere in the pursuit of your goals.

Embracing Challenges: A growth mindset encourages you to welcome challenges rather than avoid them. Challenges are seen as a necessary and valuable part of the personal growth journey in your "Selfcation" path.

Embracing challenges doesn't promote throwing yourself into hot water and jeopardise yourself. It encourages you to unleash your potential.

Adaptability: The belief that intelligence and abilities can be developed leads to increased adaptability. You are more open to trying new things and adapting to changing circumstances with a growth mindset. You realise some events are out of your control and you need to adapt yourself when they happen.

Also, it is advisable to categorise events into those that you have control over them and facts that you cannot manipulate and change them. In terms of facts, you need to accept and adopt.

Increased Effort and Persistence: A growth mindset is associated with a willingness to invest effort and persist in the face of difficulties. You are more likely to take on challenges that may initially seem daunting.

Positive View on Feedback: Feedback, whether positive or critical, is seen as valuable input for improvement. This mindset encourages a continuous feedback loop that supports ongoing personal and professional development.

In summary, adopting a growth mindset is closely tied to the pursuit of personal growth in the "Selfcation" journey. By cultivating a belief in the ability to develop and improve, you can approach challenges with resilience, view setbacks as opportunities for learning, and actively engage in the process of self-improvement. Adopting a growth mindset is a powerful drive for achieving personal and professional success.

You may get motivated by gaining more knowledge about the growth mindset, so more insights about raising the growth mindset and personal growth that can help in the "Selfcation" journey include:

Mindset Shapes Perception: Your mindset influences not only how you approach challenges but also shapes your overall perception of the world. A positive mindset can lead to a more optimistic and proactive outlook on life, bringing personal growth.

Note according to studies, too much optimism can lead to poor decision-making and lower cognitive skills. I don't promote optimism without backing it up with reality and studies' findings. Also, you need to be proactive and execute your goal-oriented tasks practically.

Mindset and Goal Setting: The type of mindset you adopt can affect the way you set and pursue goals. Individuals with a growth mindset are more likely to set ambitious yet attainable goals, viewing them as opportunities for learning and advancement.

Mindset and Relationships: Your mindset not only influences how you approach personal challenges but also plays a role in your interactions with others. A growth mindset can enhance your ability to collaborate, empathise, and build positive relationships.

The Role of Continuous Learning: A growth mindset aligns naturally with a commitment to continuous learning. Achieving new information, seeking out diverse perspectives, and staying curious are integral to the mindset that brings up personal growth.

Combining Mindset with Action: While mindset is a powerful foundation, personal growth is also about taking tangible actions. A growth-oriented mindset is most effective when paired with intentional efforts to learn, improve, and implement new insights in your daily life.

Mindset and Overcoming Limiting Beliefs: Limiting beliefs can hinder personal growth. Developing a growth mindset involves challenging and overcoming these limiting beliefs, enabling you to unlock your full potential. We will talk more about the limiting beliefs in detail in chapters 5.

In the "Selfcation" journey, first, appreciate yourself. Then, reflect on the challenges you've overcome, as well as your achievements and the lessons you've learnt from setbacks. Having said about the growth mindset, design a plan for yourself to assist you in nurturing growth mindset. You can get help from the exercises you've practiced so far, e.g. you acknowledge learning by designing such an exercise. After doing it:

Celebrating Progress: In the journey of "Selfcation", it's important to celebrate small victories and achievements. A growth mindset encourages acknowledging progress as a positive step forward, no matter how small it is. It is worth mentioning the Japanese word of Kaizen that translates to change for better or continuous improvement. The fundamental idea behind Kaizen is to make small, incremental improvements consistently over time, leading to significant positive changes in efficiency, quality, and overall performance. Remember this word to recognise your improvement.

To conclude, your mindset is a powerful force that not only influences your approach to challenges but also shapes the trajectory of your personal growth in the "Selfcation" journey. By nurturing a growth-oriented mindset, you can open doors to continuous learning, resilience, and a more fulfilling life.

In the coming chapters the growth mindset will be cultivated more, self-limiting beliefs will be traced, and finally personal growth strategies will be explained.

Chapter 4

Cultivating a Growth Mindset

In this important chapter, we continue on a transformative exploration of the concept of a growth mindset, a mental framework that holds the key to profound personal development. As we dig into the principles of this mindset, you will discover how it can reshape your approach to challenges, redefine your relationship with failure, and instill a deep belief in the power of continuous learning in your "Selfcation" journey. Here are more knowledge and insights about the growth mindset.

The Essence of the Growth Mindset: The growth mindset is more than just a mindset, it's a philosophy that fundamentally alters the way we perceive ourselves and the world around us. At its core, a growth mindset is about embracing challenges, viewing failures as stepping stones to success, and recognising that intelligence and abilities can be improved through persistence, dedication, and effort.

Cultivating a Mindset that Thrives on Challenges: Challenges and failures can be considered as threats or opportunities. Challenges are not roadblocks but growth opportunities. A growth mindset allows you to see challenges as a means to stretch your capabilities, acquire new skills, and push the boundaries of your potential. Through real-life examples and practical insights, you'll gain a deeper understanding of how challenges can become catalysts for personal and professional advancement.

Align with "Selfcation", cultivating a mindset that thrives on challenges involves intentional practices and exercises to reshape your perspective and build resilience. You are wrestling with yourself constantly to achieve your highest potential. Here are some exercises to help you develop a growth mindset that embraces challenges in your "Selfcation" journey. Take a deep breath, bring your pen and notebook, and start with the below tasks:

1. Challenge Reflection:

Regularly reflect on past challenges you faced and overcame. Identify the skills, strengths, and lessons gained from these experiences. This exercise reinforces the idea that challenges contribute to personal growth and they are growth opportunities. If you don't confront any challenges, you repeat the same routine. Challenges make you think and see from a different perspective, and encourages creativity.

Some people wonder why they face the same challenges and hardships in their lives. One possibility is that they may need to learn something from these challenges, and they should try different solutions to overcome them. They shouldn't get trapped in a loop. If challenges constantly repeat in the same manner in your life, reflect on them here. This exercise will assist you.

2. Positive Affirmations:

Create positive affirmations related to challenges. For example, "I embrace challenges as opportunities for growth" or "Every challenge I face is a chance to learn and improve". Repeat and apply these affirmations daily to reinforce a positive mindset in practice. You need to be proactive in this process; otherwise, it may seem like you are deceiving yourself and merely repeating words without backing them up with actions.

3. Goal Setting and Progress Tracking:

Set challenging but achievable goals for yourself. Break them down into smaller tasks and track your progress. Celebrate each milestone, reinforcing the idea that challenges are stepping stones towards your objectives. Remind yourself about the "Selfcation" journey that you are on to obtain sustainability in your path and mindset.

4. Comfort Zone Stretch:

Identify a specific area in your life where you've been avoiding challenges due to discomfort. Take a small step outside your comfort zone and confront the challenge. Gradually increase the difficulty to build up resilience over time. Expose yourself gradually to the area you've been avoiding, a kind of exposure technique that experts implement mostly in dealing with phobia.

5. Mindfulness Meditation for Resilience:

Another suggestion for practicing mindfulness and meditation. This time practice mindfulness meditation to develop resilience in the face of challenges. Focus on being present, acknowledging your thoughts and emotions without judgement. This can enhance your ability to respond to challenges with clarity and composure. Also, it can help in self-acceptance in your "Selfcation" journey.

6. Failure Redefinition:

Reflect on past failures and reframe your perspective. Instead of viewing them negatively, identify the lessons learnt and how they contributed to your growth. Write down your reflections to reinforce the positive aspects and learning opportunities of failure you experienced.

Rewrite the scenario that ended up in failure by implementing the lessons you learnt in that experience that led to a better ending. Editing such scenarios is a useful practice in your "Selfcation" journey.

By getting help from the list of your strengths and weaknesses that you wrote in the self-discovery and awareness section, create a list of your strengths and talents. Reflect on how they can be applied to overcome challenges. Understanding your capabilities boosts confidence and resilience when facing difficult situations.

7. Visualisation of Success:

Engage in guided visualisation exercises where you picture yourself that you overcome challenges. Visualising success can build a positive mindset and increase your confidence in your ability to thrive in the face of adversity.

Remember visualisations in mind is good, but it is not good enough during your "Selfcation" journey. You need to implement such visualisation in practice. Mere visualisation without action, is deceiving yourself.

Breakdown your visualisations picture into small steps and start taking baby steps in practice to achieve the bigger picture. Try to practice visualisation on a planned schedule. In this way, you are conditioning yourself to achieve your visualisation picture.

If you organise your schedule to do everything according to a pre-planned schedule as much as possible, your whole life will be more organised.

8. Constructive Self-Talk:

The language you use in your internal dialogue can impact your mindset significantly. Cultivating positive and growth-oriented self-talk can contribute to a healthier mindset and, consequently, support personal development and growth mindset in your "Selfcation" journey.

Develop a habit of constructive self-talk when encountering failure. Replace self-critical thoughts with affirmations that emphasise learning, growth, and the resilience gained through the experience. Withhold judgements and self-criticism.

Pay attention to your inner dialogue when facing challenges. Replace negative or self-limiting thoughts with constructive and empowering statements. Challenge negative self-talk by consciously reframing it in a more positive light.

You can seek help or combine this exercise with task number 6, which involves redefining failure.

9. Learning Mindset Journal:

Keep a journal dedicated to your learnings. Record instances where challenges led to new insights, skills, or personal growth. Use this journal to reinforce the idea that challenges are essential for continuous learning.

Reflect on your reaction after every challenge you confront and check for any similar trends in the challenges as well as your reactions.

10. Role Model Analysis:

Like the assignment in identifying values in chapter 3, identify individuals you admire who have successfully navigated challenges. Analyse your mindset and approach to difficulties. Consider how you can adopt a customised similar mindset in your "Selfcation" journey.

Remember, cultivating a mindset that thrives on challenges is an ongoing process. Consistent practice of these exercises can gradually shift your perspective, helping you approach challenges with resilience, enthusiasm, and a belief in your ability to grow through adversity.

Now we continue the list to gain more knowledge and insights about the growth mindset.

Seeing Failures as Opportunities: Failure is an inevitable part of any journey but as mentioned, a growth mindset transforms the narrative around failure to make it an opportunity for transformation, and improvement. Instead of viewing it as a dead-end, you'll learn to see failure as a valuable teacher, an opportunity to learn, adjust, and refine your approach. Embracing failure with a growth mindset becomes a powerful strategy for resilience and continuous improvement. Practical strategies in dealing with failure can help you in the "Selfcation" journey to flourish after failure. Don't close your notebook, still you need it. Below are practical strategies to assist you in seeing opportunities in failures.

1. Post-Failure Reflection:

After facing a setback, engage in a reflective process. Analyse the factors that contributed to the failure, identify lessons learnt, and consider how you can apply these insights in future endeavours.

2. Seeking Support:

Reach out to mentors, peers, or a supportive network when facing failure. Discussing the experience with others can provide additional perspectives, encouragement, and insights that contribute to the learning process.

Embrace the Transformation: After knowing about the growth mindset and how to confront failure, it is time to embrace the transformation. Embrace the Transformation is a call to willingly accept and engage in the process of significant change or development, particularly in the context of personal growth and self-improvement. This phrase contains the idea of being open, accepting, and proactive in the face of transformative experiences and opportunities.

After discussing failure, redefining setbacks, and reflecting on them, write new scenarios, etc. It's essential to bring in fresh perspectives to immerse yourself in the transformation process. Treat yourself to a delicious snack as a way to invigorate and then continue with the "Selfcation" journey. Let's break down the key elements of this concept and practice them:

1. Willingness to Change:

Embracing the transformation implies a willingness to change aspects of yourself, your mindset, or your life. As mentioned before, it acknowledges that personal growth often involves stepping outside your comfort zone, and being open to new opportunities and expose yourself to them.

Write about an activity that can echo your willingness to change.

2. Active Engagement:

In "Selfcation", it's not just about passively accepting the change; it's about actively engaging with the transformative process. This may involve setting goals, seeking new experiences, and taking intentional steps toward self-improvement.

Determine a new activity that you want to try and challenge yourself to do it.

3. Positive Attitude:

Embracing transformation requires maintaining a positive attitude, even in the face of challenges or uncertainties. It's an optimistic outlook that sees change as an opportunity for growth rather than as a threat. Remember, as mentioned before, according to studies, too much positivism leads to cognitive decline and poor decision making.

Reflect on your level of optimism or pessimism. Also, check whether they are related to the environment or the context or if they are merely person-oriented and rooted from inside.

4. Recognition of Potential:

The task suggests recognising the potential for constructive outcomes and personal development that can arise from transformative experiences. It encourages you to view change as a means to unlock your full potential. Your potential will be revealed when you are challenged in the situations you did not experience before.

Revisit the list you wrote about your strengths and talents and reflect on it.

5. Acknowledgment of the Journey:

Embracing the transformation acknowledges that personal growth is a journey, often with ups and downs. It's a recognition that the process is ongoing and that each step contributes to a larger, evolving narrative and knowledge of self-discovery that can result in a better you in your journey of the "Selfcation".

Remind yourself about your takeaways each day that can contribute in your "Selfcation" journey. No matter how small your takeaways are daily or weekly, acknowledge and recognise them.

6. Adaptability:

Being open to transformation implies a level of adaptability. It means being both flexible and resilient in the face of unexpected changes, challenges, or setbacks. Learn to flow with challenges to be able to deal with them better. Rigidity can lead to breaking more than flexibility.

Remember situations where adaptability could help you.

7. Commitment to Personal Development:

Embracing the transformation is a commitment to personal development. It signifies a conscious decision to actively work on becoming the best version of yourself and to continuously seek opportunities for improvement in the "Selfcation" journey. Below exercise is a difficult one, but it is worth starting to think about it.

Define yourself in only one word. What word defines, represents, and echoes you better.

8. Mindset Shift:

This practice aligns with the growth mindset and adaptability often involves a mindset shift from resistance to acceptance. Instead of fearing or resisting change, you are encouraged to see it as a natural and necessary part of the journey toward personal fulfillment. Adopting the growth mindset facilitates this process.

As per DBT, first you need to accept and then you can implement change interventions. First recognise your current mindset and then, try to change it to assist you in your "Selfcation" journey.

9. Empowerment:

Ultimately, embracing the transformation is an empowering concept. It places you in the driver's seat of your development, encouraging a proactive and intentional approach to life's changes and challenges in your "Selfcation" journey.

To wrap up, recognising failure with a growth mindset is a strategic approach to navigating life's challenges in the "Selfcation" journey. It transforms failure from a source of fear and threat into a catalyst for resilience, learning, and continuous improvement. The journey towards success is not a linear path; it's a dynamic, evolving process where failure, when embraced, becomes a powerful force for growth and development. Embrace the transformation is a rallying cry for you to actively and constructively engage with the process of personal growth and change. It encourages a mindset that sees transformation as an exciting and empowering journey rather than a daunting or negative experience.

Now it is time to check on the self-limiting beliefs as milestones that hider you on your development road.

Chapter 5

Navigating Self-Limiting Beliefs

Self-limiting beliefs are invisible barriers that often hold us back from reaching our full potential. In this chapter, we'll uncover the most common self-limiting beliefs and how they influence our thoughts, behaviours, and decisions. You'll gain insight into recognising these beliefs in your life and learn effective techniques to challenge and overcome them. By conquering your self-limiting beliefs, you'll unlock the door to personal growth and a future free from self-imposed limitations, and you'll be on the right path of "Selfcation".

Self-limiting beliefs are destructive thoughts and perceptions individuals hold about themselves and their abilities, which can hinder personal development and achievement. These beliefs create mental barriers that limit one's potential and can be a significant obstacle on the path to self-improvement. Here's an exploration of self-limiting beliefs in the context of personal development:

Origins of Self-Limiting Beliefs:

This statement is backed up by different psychological theories such as psychanalysis theory by Sigmund Freud and attachment theory by John Bowlby. Many self-limiting beliefs originate from early childhood experiences, interactions, or feedback received from parents, teachers, or peers. Comments like "You're not good enough" or "You can't do that" can leave lasting imprints.

Social comparisons and societal pressures contribute to self-limiting beliefs as well. Constantly measuring oneself against others or societal standards can bring up beliefs of inadequacy or a sense that certain achievements are unattainable.

Experiences of failure, especially when accompanied by negative self-talk, can lead to the adoption of self-limiting beliefs. Individuals may generalise these failures, believing they are incapable in broader aspects of life.

If you see such traces, try the backward technique. Remember the last stage of the memory and start going back to discover the oldest memory in your mind that can build self-limiting beliefs. You can go backward step-by-step. Stop when you feel a butterfly in your stomach, and again, after some time, repeat it. Gradually you get close to discovering the origin. Every time you get an insight, rewrite the scenario and practice it. This is a technique used in behaviour modifications backed up by behaviorism approach.

After reading about the potential origin of self-limiting beliefs, common self-limiting beliefs are presented here to shed light on them and challenging them:

Common Self-Limiting Beliefs:

Fear of Failure: Believing that failure is unacceptable or defines personal worth can prevent you from taking risks or pursuing challenging goals. Failure ends up in misery.

Failure doesn't define you as a person. Failure is separate from your identity and the person you are.

Impostor Syndrome: Feeling undeserving of success and fearing exposure as a fraud, even in the face of evidence of competence, is a common self-limiting belief known as impostor syndrome. It is important to know more about imposter syndrome, especially because it finds its way into daily conversations and people talk about it usually without having proper academic knowledge about it. More information about it is provided at the end of this chapter.

Perfectionism: The belief that everything must be flawless can lead to paralysis and procrastination, as the fear of not meeting impossibly high standards takes precedence and it prevents your progress.

Fixed Mindset: Believing that intelligence and abilities are fixed traits, rather than qualities that can be developed, can stifle the desire for learning and growth. By shifting your mindset to a growth mindset, you can overcome this challenge.

Catastrophising: Expecting the worst-case scenario in every situation can hinder decision-making and create unnecessary anxiety, rooted in the belief that negative outcomes are inevitable. You can consider the worst scenario as a learning opportunity and plan for dealing with potential risks and milestones on the way.

Catasrophising is one of the cognitive biases. You can check in academic sources to know more about it as well as other cognitive biases.

Knowing about the common self-limiting beliefs enables you to realise how they can impact personal development such as:

Limited Goal-Setting: Individuals with self-limiting beliefs may set goals that are easily achievable or well below their actual potential. Ambitious goals may be dismissed as unattainable.

Self-limiting beliefs may impact cognitive abilities including executive functions such as thinking, decision-making, memory, self-monitoring, planning, etc.

Risk Aversion: Fear of failure or rejection can lead to a reluctance to take risks, try new experiences, or step outside one's comfort zone, blocking personal and professional growth. You read more about risk later in this book, mostly in chapter 16.

Undermined Confidence: Self-limiting beliefs erode self-empowerment, creating a mental barrier that reinforces the idea of being incapable or unworthy of success.

Missed Opportunities: Opportunities for growth and advancement may be overlooked or dismissed due to the belief that one is not qualified or capable enough to seize them.

Lack of Resilience: Individuals with self-limiting beliefs may struggle to challenge and overcome setbacks. Each failure may be seen as confirmation of their perceived limitations, further undermining resilience.

Now is the time to find out how to overcome the self-limiting beliefs on the way to the "Selfcation". Here are some suggestions. First, take a deep breath, bring your notebook and pen, pamper yourself by a cup of tea or coffee, and then continue reading:

1.   Awareness:

Recognise and acknowledge self-limiting beliefs. Awareness is the initial step toward challenging and overcoming these destructive thought patterns. You need to recognise and, as per DBT, accept them, then you can start changing them accordingly.

Think about whether you can find similar examples of self-limiting beliefs that we are discussing here in your life. Recognising such beliefs is a key step in challenging them and working towards positive change.

2. Challenge Negative Thoughts:

Actively and intentionally challenge negative self-talk by questioning the validity of limiting beliefs. Consider evidence to the contrary and reframe thoughts in a more positive light. Constructive thought doesn't underscore a realistic view. Again, remember extreme positivist view results in cognitive decline and poor decision making as per the researches.

3. Set Realistic Goals:

Break larger goals into smaller, and more manageable steps. As it was mentioned before, achieving these incremental successes can help improving self-belief and challenge self-limiting beliefs. This reflects algorithmic thinking, i.e., step-by-step at a manageable pace.

4. Cultivate a Growth Mindset:

Again, embrace the idea that intelligence and abilities can be developed and improved through effort and learning. A growth mindset fosters a belief in your capacity for improvement.

5. Seek Support:

Share self-limiting beliefs with a trusted friend, mentor, or therapist. External perspectives can provide valuable insights and support in overcoming negative thought patterns.

You may identify repetitive sentences or words in your self-talk. Examine them to determine whether they contribute to self-limiting beliefs. If so, make an effort to replace and edit them now. Listen to your self-talk with the intention of uncovering hints and clues about your inner self.

6. Celebrate Achievements:

Like before, celebrate even small achievements. Acknowledging successes, no matter how minor, helps counteract the destructive impact of self-limiting beliefs.

If things go against your wish, you may repeatedly remind yourself and it ends up in remuneration. I encourage you to remember your achievements. If you don't do so, they may slide in the crack and fade out.

7. Continuous Learning:

Nurture a mindset of continuous learning and improvement. Embrace challenges as opportunities for growth and view setbacks as temporary obstacles on the journey to success. Consider the lessons you learnt and implement them in your future endeavours.

Remind yourself that you are on the personal development and improvement path and you are stretching your comfort-zone when you confront challenges. In addition, they are necessary tasks to do on your "Selfcation" journey to unlock your potential.

Overcoming self-limiting beliefs is an ongoing process that requires self-reflection, planning, self-monitoring, resilience, and a commitment to personal development in the "Selfcation" journey.

In the next chapter strategies for personal growth will be discussed in more detail to help you in your "Selfcation" journey, but before that as I mentioned, you find more information about imposter syndrome.

Impostor Syndrome refers to a psychological phenomenon where individuals, despite external evidence of their competence and achievements, persistently doubt their abilities and fear being exposed as may result in failures. People experiencing impostor syndrome often have a persistent internal belief that they are not as competent as others perceive them to be. This phenomenon can affect anyone, regardless of their actual accomplishments or level of expertise.

Key Features of Impostor Syndrome:

Persistent Self-Doubt: Individuals with impostor syndrome tend to doubt their skills, accomplishments, and overall worth. Despite external validation, they may believe they are undeserving of their success.

Fear of Exposure: There is a constant fear of being exposed as a fraud. Individuals may believe that others will eventually discover they are not as competent as they appear to be.

Attributing Success to External Factors: Those experiencing impostor syndrome often attribute their success to external factors such as luck, timing, or the assistance of others, discounting their own contributions and abilities.

High Standards and Perfectionism: Individuals with impostor syndrome often set unrealistically high standards for themselves and may engage in perfectionistic tendencies. This pursuit of perfection can lead to chronic dissatisfaction with their achievements.

Difficulty Internalising Success: Success and positive feedback may not be internalised. Instead of feeling a sense of accomplishment, individuals with impostor syndrome may dismiss positive outcomes as a result of luck or coincidence. The belief of failure becomes ingrained in their minds.

Overworking to Prove Worth: Some individuals with impostor syndrome may overwork or over-prepare to compensate for their perceived lack of competence. This pattern can lead to burnout and increased stress.

Types of Impostor Syndrome:

There are five different types of imposter syndrome namely:

The Perfectionist: Set extremely high standards for themselves and feel they must achieve flawlessness in everything they do. Any perceived failure is magnified and catastrophised.

The Expert: Feels the need to know everything before starting a task. Afraid of being exposed as unknowledgeable, they may be hesitant to ask questions or seek help.

The Soloist: Prefers to work alone and may avoid seeking support or collaboration. The soloist believes that asking for help will reveal their incompetence.

The Natural Genius: Expect to excel without significant effort and become frustrated or anxious when they face challenges. They fear that if they have to struggle, it means they are not truly competent.

The Superman: Feels the need to excel in all aspects of life, including career family, and personal relationships. Balancing multiple roles may lead to burnout.

Impacts:

High Achievers at Risk: Impostor syndrome often affects high-achieving individuals, including professionals, academics, and creative artists.

Cultural and Social Influences: Cultural and social factors, such as societal expectations or stereotypes related to success, can contribute to the development of impostor syndrome.

Perfectionistic Environments: Work or academic environments that emphasise perfectionism and constant achievement may build up impostor syndrome.

Early Experiences: Early experiences, such as receiving excessive praise or criticism, may contribute to the development of impostor syndrome in adulthood.

To summarise, impostor syndrome is a common experience that can be addressed through self-awareness, self-compassion, and intentional efforts to reframe negative thought patterns. Recognising your worth and abilities is crucial for developing a healthier mindset and promoting continued personal and professional development.

Now we continue to the next chapter, strategies for personal growth.

Chapter 6

Strategies for Personal Growth

Personal growth in the "Selfcation" journey is deliberate lifestyle interventions along with continuous behaviour modifications. This chapter is designed to empower you to shift your perspective, break free from self-limiting beliefs, and equip you with a range of strategies to improve your personal development. From setting meaningful goals and planning your path to honing your skills and embracing new experiences, you'll find a comprehensive guide to improving your growth. Insights and practical strategies are suggested to assist you in evolving as the best version of yourself. First, more insights are suggested and then practical exercises are put forward.

Deliberate and Continuous Personal Growth:

Deliberate and continuous personal growth refers to the intentional and ongoing process of self-improvement, development, and advancement in various aspects of your life. In the "Selfcation" journey, this approach involves purposeful actions, thoughtful planning, and a commitment to evolving and engagement over time. The key elements of deliberate and continuous personal growth can be defined as follows:

Foundations of Personal Development: Personal growth is considered as a deliberate and continuous process, acknowledging that it is not a destination but a journey of ongoing improvement toward the "Selfcation". You can enjoy the path scenery and adventures. Don't wait till you reach the destination. You're on the way, kudos to you. Recognise and celebrate it.

Intentionality in Goal Setting: Goal setting is presented as a foundational aspect of personal growth. The academic exploration adds to the psychology of goal-setting, emphasising the importance of setting meaningful, challenging but achievable objectives. More about the meaningful goals will be explained in the chapter 7.

Strategic Path Planning: The concept of planning your path for personal development involves creating a strategic roadmap that aligns with you values, aspirations, and the principles of the "Selfcation" and the growth mindset.

Skill Development as a Continuous Process: Skill development as a continuous process refers to the ongoing and deliberate refinement and enhancement of your abilities, competencies, and expertise over time. It involves a proactive and lifelong commitment to acquiring new skills, polishing existing ones, and adapting to changing demands and challenges. The process of skill development is not a one-time event but rather a dynamic journey that requires consistent effort, learning, and adaptation throughout your life.

Experiential Learning: Experiential learning involves acquiring knowledge and skills through direct, obtaining hands-on skills through experiences. It emphasises learning by doing, reflecting on those experiences, and applying insights gained to enhance personal growth. It recognises that practical, real-world encounters provide valuable opportunities for you to expand your perspectives, develop new abilities, and deepen your understanding of yourself and the world around you. Also, you can build up the appropriate know-how skills in your "Selfcation".

Comprehensive Guide to Nurture Growth: A comprehensive guide to fostering growth in personal development serves as a thorough and inclusive resource that offers insights, strategies, and practical advice to support you in your self-improvement journey to your "Selfcation". This guide typically covers various aspects, including goal setting, mindset shifts, overcoming self-limiting beliefs, skill development, and embracing new experiences. It provides a holistic approach, drawing on a range of proven strategies and techniques grounded in research and psychology to empower you to evolve continually as the best version of yourself. A few of such strategies and techniques include adaptability, skill development, embracing new experiences, and resilience in the face of setbacks that we talked about.

Empowering Perspectives and Strategies:

Empowering perspectives and strategies in the "Selfcation" journey of personal development involves adopting positive and constructive viewpoints while implementing actionable techniques to enhance your growth and well-being. You need to recognise, learn, implement practically, reflect, and again recognise, learn, implement practically, and reflect. Remember this sequence all through your "Selfcation" journey.

Empowering perspectives and strategies in personal development focus on cultivating constructive growth mindsets, challenging limiting beliefs, and providing actionable approaches to improve continuous growth. These approaches empower you to take control of your development, navigate challenges with resilience, and hit the road of a transformative journey of self-improvement toward "Selfcation".

Now is time for the practical exercises. Bring your notebook and pen, take a deep breath, and start with the below suggestions:

1. Mindset Shift:

As mentioned in chapter 4, instead of viewing challenges as blockages, adopt a growth mindset that sees challenges as opportunities for learning and growth. Embrace the belief that abilities can be developed through effort and persistence.

Remember a setback you experienced and try to consider a constructive perspective to it and write down about the lessons you can learn from it. Embrace challenges as learning opportunities. Instead of avoiding difficult tasks, approach them with curiosity and withhold judgement about the result. In chapter 7, the concept and meaning and searching for meaning will be discussed backed up by the academic theory of logotherapy.

2. Breaking Free from Self-Limiting Beliefs:

Challenge the self-limiting beliefs by acknowledging accomplishments, recognising strengths, and reframing destructive thoughts with constructive affirmations.

The same event you remembered in the previous task, recognise potential self-limiting beliefs. Write them down and try to replace them by constructive statements and practical tasks to overcome them. Also, tackle how they hinder your improvement.

Overcome self-limiting beliefs by what you learnt in the previous chapter, challenge the belief that "I'm not creative" by engaging in creative activities regularly. This might include writing, drawing, or exploring new hobbies to nurture a more positive self-perception.

3. Equipping with Practical Strategies:
Prepare yourself with specific, actionable tools such as goal-setting frameworks, time management techniques, and mindfulness practices to apply in your daily life for tangible personal and professional growth.
If you wrote about them in previous exercises, review and edit them if needed. If you didn't write about any of the above-mentioned strategies, write them now.

4. Strategic Goal Setting:

Set a SMART goal such as "I will complete a professional development course within the next three months". This provides a clear and achievable target for personal growth. SMART is the acronym of:

Specific: Clearly define what you want to achieve.

Measurable: Establish criteria for tracking your progress and determining when the goal is achieved.

Achievable: Ensure that the goal is hard enough, but realistic and attainable, considering your resources and constraints.

Relevant: Make sure the goal is meaningful and aligned with your overall aspirations and values.

Time-bound: Set a deadline or timeframe to create a sense of urgency and prevent procrastination.

Spend more time here and determine your SMART strategic goals. These parameters can help you to pertain to your goals in your "Selfcation" journey. You revisit them while you're gaining more knowledge and information.

5. Overcoming Self-Limiting Beliefs:

By what you learnt in the previous chapter, challenge the belief that "I'm not creative" by engaging in creative activities regularly. This might include writing, drawing, or exploring new hobbies to nurture a more positive self-perception.

6. Continuous Learning and Skill Development:
Enroll in a course to acquire new skills or enhance existing ones. Actively seeking learning opportunities empowers you to stay relevant and adaptable in your personal and professional lives and align with your values and goals. They can be additive to your personal development in your "Selfcation" journey.

7. Reflective Practices:

Establish a daily journaling practice to reflect on experiences, emotions, and personal insights. Regular self-reflection empowers you to gain a deeper understanding of yourself and your goals. In addition, it helps you to express yourself better.

Furthermore, your self-monitoring, planning skills, and, essentially, your cognitive abilities will be polished as well. The more you practice, the deeper the pathways in your neural system will become to engrave personal improvement.

Reflect on your responses to the previous exercises of this chapters.

8. Resilience Building:

When you face a setback, focus on what can be learnt from the experience rather than dwelling on the failure. This shift in perspective empowers you to bounce back stronger and prepare yourself for another trial.

Collect your mind and focus on here and now and reflect on your current status on resilience spectrum. Imagine an arbitrary situation and try to manage it and rate your performance in it.

9. Holistic Well-Being:

Prioritise self-care by incorporating regular exercise, adequate sleep, and moments of relaxation into daily routines. A holistic approach to well-being empowers you to thrive in various aspects of your life. In chapters 12 and 13 self-care will be explored more. Put a reminder for yourself that you need to insert more 'me-time' in your daily schedule.

These assignments illustrate how empowering perspectives and strategies can be integrated into daily life, fostering a growth mindset, resilience, and continuous personal growth in the "Selfcation" journey. One of the common issues people confront is adhering to their goals to achieve them. In the coming chapter setting and pursuing goals will be discussed in more detail to assist you to adhere to your goals in your "Selfcation" journey.

What you get by achieving your goals is not as important as what you become by achieving your goals.

Zig Ziglar

4. Setting and Pursuing Goals

S etting and pursuing goals is a fundamental aspect of personal development as well as providing a structured framework for growth and achievement in the "Selfcation". In the current section, guidance on how to effectively set and pursue goals will be presented, and then, providing a structured framework for growth and achievement, creating a personal development plan, and staying motivated and focused will be discussed. These concepts are not isolated and they impact each other and they are interrelated.

Setting Goals:

Follow SMART Framework:

SMART framework was introduced in the chapter 6. Here just a quick reminder of this acronym as Specific, Measurable, Achievable, and Relevant, and Time-bound.

Pursuing Goals:

Some assignments are reminded to assist you to achieve your goals:

1. Break Down into Smaller Tasks:

Divide larger goals into smaller and more manageable tasks. This makes the overall goal less overwhelming and allows you to achieve them and acknowledge achievements along the way.

Achievement bring feeling of satisfaction. It is good to write down your goals in 'To Do List' format. Break them down and write their breakdowns and mark achieved after each one that is fulfilled.

2. Create an Action Plan:

Develop a step-by-step action plan outlining the specific tasks and milestones to reach your goal. Having a roadmap enhances clarity and guides your efforts. Also, it can prepare you for potential hinders on your way in advance.

3. Stay Consistent:

Consistency is key to goal pursuit. Establish regular routines and habits that support your objectives. Small, consistent efforts over time lead to significant results. Consistency associated with persistence. Once these two are paired with each other, adhering to your goals and achieving them becomes more manageable.

4. Monitor Progress:

Regularly assess your progress towards your goals. This could involve keeping a journal, using tracking apps, or holding periodic check-ins to evaluate your achievements and make adjustments if required. You need to constantly observe and self-monitor your progress.

5. Adaptability:

Be flexible and willing to adjust your goals based on changing circumstances. Life is dynamic, and being adaptable ensures that your goals remain realistic and achievable and reflect your self-development pathway. With adaptability, you don't feel left behind; instead, you experience a sense of inclusion in today's world.

6. Learn from Setbacks:

Analyse what went wrong, adjust your approach as needed, and use the knowledge you've learnt so far, to improve your strategies for future goal pursuit. Refer to the failure redefinition assignment in chapter 4 and reflect on it.

7. Review and Reflect:

Periodically review your goals and reflect on your progress. Evaluate whether your objectives remain relevant and adjust them accordingly. This reflective practice ensures that your goals align with your evolving aspirations.

By setting well-defined and achievable goals, and implementing effective strategies for pursuit, you create a roadmap for personal development in the "Selfcation" journey. This intentional approach to goal-setting and pursuit contributes to continuous growth and success in various aspects of your life and situate you on the personal development path. You should be conscious about the goals you set for yourself. They should be aligned with your values and aspiration. Also, they should be meaningful. Now you are prepared to dive into setting and achieving meaningful goals.

Chapter 7

Setting and Achieving Meaningful Goals

G oals serve as the compass of our lives, guiding us toward our desired destinations. In this chapter, we'll dig into the art of setting meaningful and achievable goals. You'll learn how to identify your core objectives, break them down into actionable steps, and create a clear roadmap for success. By the end of this chapter, you'll be equipped with the skills to set meaningful goals that resonate with your aspirations and the strategies to turn them into reality.

In the world of psychotherapy, talking about meaning is associated with the neurologist and psychiatrist Viktor Frankl. He suggested logotherapy, which is based on the premise that the primary motivational force of a human being is to find meaning in life. We do not dig into the philosophy and details of logotherapy, but it is good to know that logotherapy serves as the foundation for meaningful goals in this book. Logotherapy is based on the belief that the search for meaning, even amidst misery, can constitute a potential solution to human suffering.

In setting and achieving meaningful goals based on logotherapy, implicitly, the mind-body connection calls for attention. While logotherapy does not directly prescribe specific mind-body techniques or exercises, its emphasis on meaning and the interconnection of psychological and physiological aspects indirectly acknowledges the importance of a holistic approach to health. Mind and body impact each other and they are correlated and interrelated. Mind-body connection will be explained more in chapter 14 and 15.

Below is the elaboration on the key components of setting and achieving meaningful goals:

Significance of Goals:

Goals are portrayed as the compass of your life, emphasising your pivotal role in navigating your path. This sets the stage for understanding the importance of having a direction and purpose. Keep in mind the concept of free will, a cornerstone accepted by logotherapy. In this framework, we actively decide on our goals and, more broadly, shape our lives. In the next chapter choice theory will be introduced that shed light on our choices.

Fasten your seatbelt and take the driver's seat of your life. You, and only you, bear the responsibility of your life. Whatever happens, you should be accountable and liable for it.

1.   Setting Meaningful Goals:

In the same realm we talk about, the concept of meaningful goals, emphasises the importance of aligning goals with your core objectives and values. It encourages you to reflect on what truly matters to you.

You wrote about your goals. The most recent one refers back to the previous chapter when SMART concept was introduced. Review and reflect on them.

2.   Actionable Steps:

The art of goal-setting involves breaking down overarching objectives into actionable steps. You need to dissect your aspirations into manageable tasks, making the pursuit of goals less overwhelming.

Design daily small steps toward your goals.

3.   Creating a Clear Roadmap:

 It is necessary to create a clear roadmap for success. It introduces the idea of strategic planning, illustrating how a well-defined path enhances clarity and facilitates progress toward goals. In this way, you can recognise and navigate intrusive thoughts and distractions. In statics words intrusive thoughts are considered as nuisance variables. Once you recognise and navigate them, you can remove them or at least reduce their impacts.

4.   Equipping with Skills:

You need to identify core objectives, honing in on what truly matters to you. This involves self-reflection and an exploration of personal values, passions and aspirations. Don't forget to obtain appropriate know-how-skills.

Ponder and play with me. Imagine you lose everything you have. What is the last thing you would lose, i.e., what would you stick to until the last moment? It may guide you to find out your life's meaning.

5. Turning Goals into Reality:

The focus shifts to turning goals into reality. It equips you with practical strategies for goal achievement, emphasising the transition from conceptualisation to actionable steps, i.e. realisation of your goals. Start with small steps, observe how far you've come, and be proud of yourself and give yourself affirmation because of your progress. Take steps in manageable pace.

6. Skills for Goal Setting:

The skills required for effective goal setting, highlight the resonance with your aspirations. Goals are presented as more than mere objectives; they are extensions of personal desires and ambitions. Listen to yourself. Hear yourself. Open up. Don't let things pile up till they blow.

7. Empowerment through Goal Setting:

Goal setting encourages a sense of agency and ownership over your journey of personal development toward "Selfcation".

Check your status against the fundamental psychological needs of a human being, i.e., autonomy, competency, and communication. Also, assess the level of agency you possess about these needs. Aim to bring and shift the locus of control internally as much as you can rather than remaining externally.

By setting and achieving meaningful goals, your life path is clearer than before. Now you create a personal development plan to adhere to in the "Selfcation" journey. Kick-off to pave your pathway.

Chapter 8

Creating a Personal Development Plan

A well-structured plan is essential for ensuring you make consistent progress on your personal growth journey of the "Selfcation". This chapter will guide you through the process of creating a personalised development plan that lines up with your goals, values, and vision for the future. We'll discuss the importance of assessing your current status, defining your objectives, and outlining the actions required to achieve them. You'll leave this chapter with a concrete plan that empowers you to take deliberate and intentional steps toward your desired outcomes.

To academically support the content of this chapter, Reality Therapy is implemented that is introduced by William Glasser. This approach views a person's behaviours as choices. According to Glasser's theory, psychological symptoms are not solely the result of mental health conditions but rather consequences of unfulfilled basic needs. Glasser is renowned for his proposed theory known as Choice Theory. To gain a comprehensive understanding, it is advisable to delve into both Choice Theory and Reality Therapy that are both introduced by Glasser, do not leave one unexplored.

Let's explain the key components in creating a personal development plan through relevant assignments that you can implement and apply in your daily life:

1. Assessing Your Current Status:

Begin by reflecting on your current situation, both personally and professionally. Consider your strengths, weaknesses, talents, skills, and areas for improvement. Refer to the lists you prepared in the previous exercises, e.g those in section 2 Self-Discovery and Awareness.

Evaluate your current habits, mindset, and lifestyle. Identify aspects of your life that contribute positively to your well-being and those that may hinder your progress. Take stock of your achievements, experiences, and lessons learned so far. This self-awareness will form the foundation for you development plan.

To assess your current state, you can implement the following academic assignments:

Self-Reflection: Take time to introspect on your values, passions, and interests. Consider what brings you joy and fulfillment.

SWOT Analysis: Identify your Strengths, Weaknesses, Opportunities you have, as well as Threats. Knowing your strengths allows you to leverage them, while addressing weaknesses enables growth rather than being a hindrance on your growth path. The same applies for opportunities and threats as well.

Life Audit: Examine different areas of your life such as career, relationships, health, and personal development. Assess what is working well and what needs improvement.

2. Defining Your Objectives:

Clearly articulate your short-term and long-term goals. These goals should align with your values and aspirations.

Break down your objectives into specific, measurable, achievable, relevant, and time-bound (SMART) targets, that we explained in chapter 6. This ensures that your goals are well-defined and manageable. Having done it, you can benefit from the following assignments to define your objectives more clearly:

Clarity in Goals: Clearly define your goals. If, for example, your goal is career advancement, specify the position you aim for and the skills required. Consider all available and potential choices you have and evaluate them.

Prioritisation: If you have multiple goals, prioritise them based on their significance and feasibility. This ensures you focus on what matters the most.

3. Outlining Actions Required:

Identify the specific actions and steps needed to achieve each of your goals. These actions should be practical, realistic, and within your control. Consider the resources, skills, and support systems required for each action. This helps in creating a roadmap that is feasible and adaptable to your circumstances.

Here are some exercises to assist you in outlining the required actions:

Break It Down: Like before, divide each goal into small actionable steps. For instance, if your goal is to learn a new skill, break it down into researching courses, setting study schedules, and adhering to regular participation in the course.

Resource Identification: Identify the resources needed for each action. This includes time, mentors, educational materials, etc.

Adaptability: Recognise that plans may need adjustment. Be open to adapting your actions based on feedback, changing circumstances, or new opportunities. Also, adapt to potential milestones and hindrances that may pop up on your way.

In this task, you realise that your journey roadmap becomes more specific and detailed paired with actions.

4. Aligning with Values and Vision:

Ensure that your personal development plan lines up with your core values. Your values serve as guiding principles that shape your decisions and actions.

Connect your plan to your broader vision for the future. How does each goal contribute to the overall vision you have for yourself? In this regard, you can practice the following tasks:

Values Assessment: Clearly define your values. If growth, integrity, and family are important to you, ensure your goals and actions align with these principles.

Vision Connection: Understand how each goal contributes to your broader vision. This connection provides a sense of purpose and motivation during challenging times and will keep you on the track.

5. Concrete Plan Empowering Deliberate Steps:

Your plan should provide clarity on the specific steps you need to take. Break down these steps into smaller, manageable tasks. This prevents overwhelm and allows for a step-by-step approach.

Establish a timeline and deadline for each task or goal. This adds a sense of agency and accountability to your plan.

Regularly review and adjust your plan as needed. Flexibility is essential as circumstances may change.

6.   Consistent Progress and Personal Empowerment:

The ultimate goal of the plan is to facilitate consistent progress and empower you to take intentional steps toward your desired outcomes.

Stay committed to the plan and track your progress regularly through self-monitoring and reflection. Celebrate achievements, learn from setbacks, and make necessary adjustments.

Accountability: Share your plan with a friend, a mentor, or a coach. Having someone to be accountable to, can increase commitment.

Adaptability: Life is dynamic, and plans may need adjustments as mentioned above. Be flexible and willing to monitor and adapt as circumstances change. Practice flow that is explained in the next chapter for adaptability. You challenge yourself to stretch your comfort zone to reach your highest potential and unlock your capabilities.

By incorporating these detailed elements into your personalised development plan, you create a comprehensive and dynamic roadmap that not only addresses your current state and goals but also adapts to the evolving nature of your personal growth in the "Selfcation" journey in the future. To keep yourself accountable for all the above-mentioned tasks, you need to keep yourself motivated and focused. The next chapter discusses how to stay motivated and focused in the "Selfcation" journey.

Before delving into discussions about motivation and focus, take a moment to contemplate and reflect on your health and well-being. Step by step, with intention, I aim to assist you in aligning with your life purpose. In simpler terms, fully engage in and embrace your life. Treat yourself with a snack. Then, complete the assignment below before moving on to the next chapter:

Healthy Lifestyle Challenge:

Think about the past week and consider how you prioritised your health. Let's rephrase it: How many times did you consciously acknowledge the importance of taking care of your health and what you did for it? Now, extend this reflection to the past month.

From this point onward, set a weekly or monthly challenge focused on cultivating healthy habits, such as exercise, nutrition, and sleep. Keep track of your progress and take time to reflect on how these changes positively impact your overall well-being.

These small adjustments in your lifestyle serve as incremental steps toward a healthier way of living, contributing to your journey of becoming a better version of yourself during your "Selfcation" adventure.

Close your eyes and visualise your better version after completing the healthy lifestyle challenge. Open your eyes when you are ready to hit the road to learn about staying motivated and focused.

Chapter 9

Staying Motivated and Focused

Maintaining motivation and focus is often the key to goal achievement. In this chapter, we'll explore effective strategies to stay motivated and overcome common obstacles that can derail your progress. We'll discuss the power of habits, the role of accountability, and the significance of a positive environment in sustaining your momentum. By the end of this chapter, you'll be well-prepared to keep your motivation high and your focus unwavering as you work towards your personal and professional goals.

Before talking about strategies to keep your motivation and focus high, we search through the concept of motivation. The underpinning theory that I use about motivation is Abraham Maslow's motivation theory which is known as the hierarchy of needs.

Maslow proposed that human needs can be arranged in a hierarchical order, with lower-level needs taking precedence over higher-level ones. The hierarchy is often represented as a pyramid and includes five levels:

Physiological Needs: These are the basic necessities for survival, such as food, water, shelter, and sleep.

Safety Needs: Once physiological needs are met, individuals seek safety and security, including health, employment, and a stable environment.

Social Needs: After safety needs, people crave social connections and a sense of belonging. This involves relationships, friendship, and being part of a community.

Esteem Needs: Once social needs are satisfied, individuals seek recognition, respect, and a sense of accomplishment. This includes self-esteem and the esteem of others.

Self-Actualisation: At the pinnacle of the hierarchy, individuals strive for self-actualisation realising their full potential, pursuing personal growth, and achieving personal goals.

Maslow's theory suggests that individuals progress through these levels in a sequential manner, with higher-level needs becoming motivating factors only after lower-level needs are met.

Over time, scholars and researchers have expanded upon or modified Maslow's original hierarchy of needs. Some variations include additional needs or reorganise the hierarchy. One notable adaptation is the inclusion of cognitive and aesthetic needs, proposed by later psychologists:

Cognitive Needs: This category involves the need for knowledge, understanding, and exploration. It reflects the desire for intellectual stimulation, curiosity, and the pursuit of meaning.

Aesthetic Needs: This need relates to the appreciation of beauty, balance, and form. It encompasses the desire for order, symmetry, and aesthetically pleasing experiences.

It's important to note that these additions are not universally accepted, and Maslow's original hierarchy remains a foundational framework for understanding human motivation. Different researchers and theorists may introduce variations based on their perspectives and observations. While Maslow's hierarchy of needs is often presented as a sequential progression, it's important to recognise that individuals may not always follow a strictly linear path. Some people might bypass lower-level needs and directly strive to satisfy higher-level needs. Let's talk about the next theory about motivation.

Vroom's Expectancy Theory focuses on individuals' expectations and beliefs regarding the outcomes of their efforts. The theory proposes that people are motivated to act in a certain way based on three key factors:

Expectancy: This refers to the belief that one's efforts will lead to a desired performance level. In other words, individuals assess whether they can successfully accomplish a task and achieve the expected performance.

Instrumentality: Instrumentality involves the belief that successful performance will result in certain outcomes or rewards. Individuals evaluate whether their performance will be rewarded and if those rewards are desirable

Valence: Valence is the value or importance an individual places on the anticipated rewards. It reflects the subjective attractiveness or desirability of the outcomes associated with successful performance.

According to Vroom, motivation is a product of these three factors multiplied by each other. Basically, as per Vroom's expectancy theory, individuals are motivated to put effort into a task if they believe they can perform well (expectancy), if they expect performance to lead to desired outcomes (instrumentality), and if they value those outcomes (valence). The theory helps explain why people choose certain behaviours and actions based on their expectations of the outcomes associated with those behaviours.

Take a deep breath and try to implement the above-mentioned theories in real life in your mind. Once you're ready, let's dive deeper into the related assignments that help in this regard:

1.   Power of Habits:

First, we start off by definition of habit to know what we are talking about. A habit is a regular behaviour or routine that becomes automatic over time. It is often performed without much conscious thought. Habits can be both beneficial, like brushing your teeth every morning and night, or less helpful, like biting your nails when stressed. They are formed through repetition and can be challenging to change once established. They engrave their pathways in your nervous system. Habits save us a lot of time and energy, so when it comes to changing them, they are so resilient to change. They were shaped through repetition and rewarding performance. To tackle your habits, seek cues in your emotions. Here we want to audit your habits in the "Selfcation" journey.

Routine and Consistency: Establishing a routine that aligns with your goals helps create habits. Consistent actions, even if small, contribute significantly over time.

Keystone Habits: Identify keystone habits, those that, when practiced consistently, have a positive impact on other areas of your life. For instance, regular exercise often leads to improved health and mental status.

Visual Cues: Use visual cues or reminders to reinforce habits. This could be a checklist, a vision board, or daily affirmations to keep your goals at the forefront of your mind.

2. Role of Accountability:

Accountability is the responsibility to answer your actions and decisions. It involves being answerable and transparent about your choices and their outcomes.

Accountability Partners: Like before, e.g. in chapter 8 consistent progress and personal empowerment, share your goals with someone you trust, such as a friend, family member, or mentor. Having someone aware of your objectives provides a sense of accountability.

Regular Check-ins: Schedule regular check-ins with your accountability partner. Discuss progress, challenges, and strategies for improvement.

Public Commitment: Consider making your goals public, whether through social media or a blog. The public commitment can enhance your sense of responsibility.

3. Significance of a Positive Environment:

Surround Yourself with Positivity: Create an environment that nurture positivity. This includes both physical spaces and the people you spend time with. Positive influences can contribute to a more optimistic as well as a growth mindset.

Limit Negative Influences: Identify and minimise exposure to negative influences or distractions. This may involve setting boundaries with certain individuals, managing your time effectively, or creating a conducive workspace.

Celebrate Successes: Acknowledge and celebrate your achievements regardless of size. Positive reinforcement encourages continued effort and helps combat feelings of stagnation.

4. Motivational Strategies:

Visualisation: Picture yourself achieving your goals. Visualisation can enhance motivation by making the desired outcome more tangible and real. If there was no hinders, what would you do. Do it now or mock the action.

Break Down Goals: As mentioned before, large goals can be overwhelming. Break them down into smaller, more manageable tasks. Completing these tasks provides a sense of accomplishment, fueling motivation.

Intrinsic Motivation: Identify the intrinsic reasons behind your goals. Connecting with personal values and passions makes the pursuit more meaningful and sustainable. This is aligned with internal locus of control that we discuss in chapter 7 in empowerment through goal setting.

5. Overcoming Common Obstacles:

Learn from Setbacks: Quick reminder, instead of viewing setbacks as failures, see them as opportunities for learning and improvement. Analyse why setback happened, adjust your approach, and move forward.

Flexibility and Adaptability: Flexibility is paramount in navigating life's dynamic journey. Embrace adaptability by remaining open to adjusting your strategies and goals as circumstances evolve. Recognise that unexpected challenges are inevitable, and the ability to pivot when necessary is a powerful asset.

By staying flexible, you not only overcome obstacles more effectively but also seize new opportunities that may arise along the way. In the ever-changing landscape of life, flexibility and adaptability become a key driver for sustained progress and success and in this way being focused plays a vital role.

In psychology, there isn't a single overarching theory specifically dedicated to the concept of focus, but there are several psychological theories and concepts that touch upon aspects related to being focused through attention and concentration. Flow Theory was selected in this book.

Flow theory, proposed by psychologist Mihaly Csikszentmihalyi, describes a mental state of complete absorption and heightened focus in an activity. This state, known as flow, is characterised by a deep sense of enjoyment and optimal performance. Key features of flow include clear goals, concentration, loss of self-consciousness, immediate feedback, balance between skills and challenge, and sense of control.

Flow is experienced in a variety of activities, such as sports, music, work, or creative endeavours. Csikszentmihalyi's research suggests that experiencing flow contributes to increased happiness, creativity, and overall well-being. The concept has been influential in fields like positive psychology, where researchers explore factors that contribute to a fulfilling and meaningful life.

Remember that the key is to find activities that strike the right balance between your current skill level and the challenges presented by the task you do. Additionally, maintaining a clear sense of purpose and immersing yourself fully in the chosen activity will enhance your chances of experiencing flow.

Below suggestions assist you to experience flow and being more focused in your daily life. Get your act together and start:

1. Creative Writing:

Set aside dedicated time for creative writing. Choose a topic or prompt, and allow your thoughts to flow onto paper without worrying about perfection.

2. Playing a Musical Instrument:

Practice playing a musical instrument, focusing on challenging pieces that match your skill level. The immersive nature of playing music can lead to a flow state.

If you don't play a musical instrument, try immersing yourself in a piece of music by listening to it to experience a flow state.

3. Drawing or Painting:

Engage in visual arts by drawing or painting. Experiment with different techniques and styles, and let your creativity guide you. Get your hands dirty and unleash your inner artist.

4. Physical Exercise or Sports:

Participate in a physical activity or sport that you enjoy. The combination of skill and challenge, along with the focus required, can lead to a flow experience.

5. Puzzle Solving:

Solve challenging puzzles, such as crosswords, Sudoku, or jigsaw puzzles. The continuous engagement with the problem-solving process can induce flow.

6. Photography:

Go out with a camera and focus on capturing moments or scenes that inspire you. The combination of technical skills and creativity can lead to a flow state.

7. Cooking or Baking:

Choose a new and somewhat challenging recipe to try. The process of preparing a meal or baking can become an absorbing and enjoyable activity.

8. Learning a New Skill:

Pick up a new skill or hobby that you find interesting, such as learning a language, a musical instrument, or a form of dance.

By incorporating these strategies into your daily life, you create a supportive framework that sustains your motivation and focus over the long term.

Remember, maintaining motivation is an ongoing process that requires planning, self-monitoring, dedication, flexibility, and adaptability. Regularly revisiting your goals, adjusting your strategies, remembering Kaizen, and celebrating successes will contribute to a sustained sense of momentum on your personal and professional journey. Relationships and communication have been discussed scatteredly so far. The next chapter is dedicated to relationships and communication.

Sometimes the easiest way to solve a problem is to stop participating in the problem.

Albert Einstein

5. Relationships and Communication

Relationships refer to connections and interactions between people here, involving emotional bonds, shared experiences, and mutual understanding. Communication means the exchange of information, thoughts, or feelings through verbal and non-verbal means, fostering understanding and connection between individuals. By knowing these brief definitions, you get the hang of things discussed in this section. Let's start by exploring building strong and authentic connections, effective communication and conflict resolution, and finally "Selfcation" approach to relationships.

In a simple categorisation, we have relationships and connections with ourselves, with others, with a superpower whatever we named this entity, and nature and animals. Keep in mind that relationship and connection don't refer only to our relationships and connections with other human beings, but here we discuss the relationships and connections with other people solely.

Chapter 10

Building Strong and Authentic Connections

Meaningful relationships are pillars of a fulfilling life. In this chapter, we'll explore the art of building strong, authentic connections with others. You'll learn the importance of genuine communication, active listening, and empathy in forming and maintaining relationships. We'll discuss strategies for developing deeper connections with friends, family, colleagues, and partners. By the end of this chapter, you'll be equipped to nurture and grow the relationships that enrich your life in "Selfcation".

To build and sustain strong and authentic connections, you need to understand and implement essential elements such as genuine communication, active listening, and empathy. The below explanations shed light on them:

Genuine Communication: Genuine communication involves expressing yourself honestly and authentically. This means being true to your thoughts, feelings, and intentions. Also, it requires clarity in expressing ideas, as well as the ability to articulate emotions and concerns openly.

In addition, avoidance of misunderstandings and misinterpretations is a key to genuine communication emphasising the importance of unambiguous communication.

Active Listening: This concept implies not just hearing the words someone is saying but truly understanding and engaging with the message. Active listening involves giving your full attention, asking clarifying questions, and showing genuine interest in what the other person is expressing. More will be explained about active listening in the coming chapter.

Empathy: Understanding and sharing the feelings of others is crucial for building meaningful connections. Empathy involves putting yourself in someone else's shoes, recognising their emotions, and responding with compassion and understanding. Recognising and acknowledging the emotions of others without judgement is a key component of empathy.

Empathy ensures that you maintain boundaries, allowing others to explore their experiences without you becoming overly involved or biased. This distinction helps you provide effective support while empowering you to navigate your emotions.

Here you find suggestions to implement your learning in your relationships.

1. Strategies for Deeper Connections:

Building deeper connections may involve spending quality time together, engaging in shared activities, and creating shared experiences. Trust-building strategies, such as being reliable and consistent, are likely to be explored. Keep in mind that different types of relationships (friends, family, colleagues, partners) may require different approaches. Rather than spending quality time together, this could involve fostering trust and creating a supportive and positive environment.

2. Nurturing and Growing Relationships:

The ultimate goal is to equip you with the tools and insights to nurture and cultivate the relationships that bring value to your lives. This might involve ongoing effort, mutual support, and adaptability to the changing dynamics of relationships over time. Moreover, strategies for resolving conflicts, maintaining a positive atmosphere, and celebrating shared achievements may be addressed.

Addressing conflicts through effective communication and compromise, maintaining a positive atmosphere through supportive communication and expressions of gratitude, and celebrating shared achievements by acknowledging and rejoicing in each other's successes are essential strategies for nurturing and strengthening meaningful relationships. These practices contribute to the overall health and satisfaction within interpersonal connections.

3. Don't Leave any Kinds of Relationships Unnoticed:

This reflects self-awareness and self-care as well. You need to have a holistic view of your relationships and connections. Distribute proportionate time in all kinds of relationships and connections. Such distribution changes from time to time. There is no fixed and rigid distribution.

In summary, the chapter guides you in understanding, building, and maintaining meaningful relationships by focusing on key aspects such as genuine communication, active listening, and empathy. Suggestions were offered to nurture authentic connections. The intention is to empower you to enrich your lives through the cultivation of deep and fulfilling connections with all different relationships and connections in your "Selfcation" journey.

Relationships and connections may not be without conflicts. In the next chapter, you find more about effective communication to prevent any misunderstandings. Additionally, we will discuss conflict resolution techniques to address clashes or disagreements constructively.

Chapter 11

Effective Communication and Conflict Resolution

E ffective communication is vital for any healthy relationship. In this chapter, we'll dive into the principles of clear and constructive communication. You'll gain more insights into active listening, assertiveness, and empathetic expression. We'll also explore strategies for resolving conflicts and misunderstandings respectfully and productively. By the end of this chapter, you'll have the skills to communicate more effectively and plot a route in challenging conversations with confidence.

Let's break down the elements of effective communication and conflict resolution in the context of building and maintaining healthy relationships and suggest some exercises to promote effective communication and conflict resolution:

1. Effective Communication as a Foundation:

Effective communication serves as the bedrock of any healthy relationship. It involves the exchange of thoughts, feelings, and information in a way that is clear, respectful, and constructive. The premise is that when you communicate effectively, you bring up understanding, trust, and connection with others.

Maintain a balance between what you receive and what you give. Don't overwhelm others by extra unnecessary information, thoughts, feelings, etc.

2. Principles of Clear and Constructive Communication:

Clear expression is important to minimise misunderstandings. This includes using straightforward language, avoiding ambiguity, and being explicit in conveying thoughts and feelings.

Constructive communication focuses on building up rather than tearing down. It involves offering feedback positively and helpfully, emphasising solutions over blame, and inviting a positive atmosphere in conversations.

3. Insights into Active Listening:

This involves fully engaging with the speaker, paying attention to both verbal and non-verbal cues, and demonstrating genuine interest in understanding the speaker's perspective. The role of active listening in enhancing communication by ensuring that both parties feel heard and valued should be respected. Paraphrasing and reflecting are affirmations that you are listening, you are interested, and you understand.

Ask clarifying questions to show you are actively engaged in listening. Give feedback in a nonjudgemental manner.

4. Assertiveness Expression:

Being assertive means expressing your thoughts, needs, and boundaries with confidence and clarity, without being overly passive or aggressive. One helpful assignment in this regard is Using "I" Statements. Advising the use of "I" statements to express personal feelings and needs without placing blame helps to take ownership of your emotions while maintaining a respectful tone.

Also, you can benefit from DEARMAN technique that is used in DBT for interpersonal effectiveness. DEARMAN is the acronym as below:

Describe the current situation (if necessary). Stick to the facts. Tell the person exactly what you are reacting to.

Express your feelings and opinions about the situation. Don't assume that the other person knows how you feel.

Assert yourself by asking for what you want or saying 'No' clearly. Do not assume that others will figure out what you want. Remember that others cannot read your mind.

Reinforce (reward) the person ahead of time by explaining positive effects of getting what you want or need. If necessary, also clarify the negative consequences of not getting what you want or need.

Mindfully keep your focus on your goals. Maintain your position. Don't be distracted. Don't get off the topic. Keep asking for what you want or say 'No' and express your opinion over and over and over. Just keep replaying the same thing again and again. Ignore attacks. If the other person attacks, threatens, or tries to change the subject, ignore the threats, comments, or attempts to divert you. Do not respond to attacks. Ignore distractions. Just keep making your point.

Appear confident, effective, and competent. Use a confident voice tone and physical manner; make good eye contact. No stammering, whispering, staring at the floor, retreating.

Negotiate and be willing to give to get. Offer and ask for other solutions to the problem. Reduce your request. Say no, but offer to do something else or to solve the problem another way. Focus on what will work.

5. Empathetic Expression:

This involves expressing yourself in a way that shows an understanding of the other person's feelings and perspectives. It contributes to creating an emotionally supportive environment.

Withhold judgement in your empathetic expression.

Active listening and random acts of kindness can assist in demonstrating empathetic expression.

Now we move to the strategies for resolving conflicts and misunderstandings.

1. Misunderstanding Resolution:

Recognising misunderstandings are a natural part of communication that can be prevented and resolved through the following practices:

Clarification Techniques: Seeking clarification during conversations to ensure that messages are accurately understood.

Ask questions and confirm your interpretation of the information. Active listening can help in this regard as well.

Open Communication Practices: Encouraging an open and transparent communication environment where you feel comfortable expressing your thoughts and seeking clarification without fear of judgement.

Reflective Practices: Promoting self-reflection on your communication style and potential sources of misunderstandings. Consider how your words and actions may be perceived by others.

Resolution through Dialogue: Guiding resolving misunderstandings through constructive dialogue rather than confrontation. This involves approaching conflicts with a problem-solving attitude and seeking mutual understanding.

Learning Opportunities: Framing misunderstandings as opportunities for learning and personal growth. View these instances not as failures but as chances to improve communication skills and deepen understanding.

2. Confidence in Challenging Conversations:

This involves not only effective communication but also the ability to manage emotions, stay focused on the topic at hand, and work towards resolution. Emotional regulation in DBT can be beneficial. Remember, consistent practice is key to developing and strengthening emotion regulation skills. It's often helpful to work with a mental health professional to tailor these exercises to your specific needs and circumstances. Below some suggested to provided:

Identify and Label Emotions: Take some time each day to identify and label your emotions. Use a feelings chart if needed. In addition, journal about your emotions, describing what triggered them and how they manifest in your body.

Mindfulness Meditation: Practice mindfulness meditation to stay present in the moment. Focus on your breath and observe your thoughts and feelings without judgement.

Opposite Action: Identify an emotion you want to change and consider its opposite. Act in a way that is consistent with the opposite emotion, e.g. if you're feeling withdrawn and sad, try engaging in activities that usually bring joy or connection.

Self-Soothing Techniques: Develop a list of self-soothing activities that help you calm down. This could include listening to music, taking a warm bath, or practicing deep-breathing exercises. Experiment with different activities to see what works best for you.

Check the Facts: Evaluate the accuracy of your thoughts and interpretations related to a specific emotion. Challenge and reframe any distorted thinking patterns contributing to the intensity of your emotions.

Build Mastery: Engage in activities that make you feel competent and accomplished. This can help boost your self-esteem and regulate your emotions. Choose activities that align with your interests and skills.

ABC Please: Attend to basic health needs, such as eating well, getting enough sleep, and exercising. Build mastery by engaging in activities that give you a sense of accomplishment. Cope ahead by anticipating and preparing for potentially difficult situations.

Objectively Describe the Situation: Practice describing a situation without including interpretations or judgements. This helps in developing a more balanced and objective view of the events triggering your emotions.

Daily Pleasant Events: Schedule and engage in activities that bring you joy or a sense of accomplishment every day. Reflect on these positive experiences at the end of the day. You can pair it with the above-mentioned Opposite Action.

In summary, this chapter equipped you with a comprehensive set of communication skills. It covered the principles of clear and constructive communication, emphasises active listening, explores assertiveness and empathetic expression, and provides practical strategies for preventing and resolving conflicts and misunderstandings. The overarching goal is to enhance your ability to communicate effectively, nurturing healthy and fulfilling relationships. After knowing the principles of healthy relationships and conflict resolutions, we delve into the "Selfcation" approach to relationships in the next chapter.

Chapter 12

The "Selfcation" Approach to Relationships

The "Selfcation" approach extends beyond personal development; it also plays a vital role in nurturing relationships, i.e., as mentioned before, relationships with yourself, others, nature and animals, as well as relationships with the superpower. In this chapter, we'll discuss how adopting a "Selfcation" mindset can enhance your connections with the mentioned relationships. You'll learn the power of focusing, building, and maintaining your authentic self through such relationships. This will lead to a more satisfying life. In this chapter, you find practical suggestions to apply this approach to various aspects of your life, from family and friendships to professional relationships. Are you ready to hit the road in the "Selfcation" journey? Let's start off by breaking down the key points:

The Scope of the "Selfcation" Approach:

"Selfcation" approach goes beyond personal development. It has a broader application, extending its influence to various aspects of life beyond individual growth. It enhances your mental capacity and encourages you to think outside the box. Challenge yourself to see from perspectives you've never considered before.

Additionally, like growth mindset, "Selfcation'" views failure and setbacks as learning opportunities. It emphasises taking a step forward, even in the face of setbacks. In the "Selfcation" approach there are two factors that can dance together harmoniously and complement each other, i.e., vulnerability and courage. Finding the right rhythm for their dance may be challenging, but patience is the key. The payoff is worthwhile. Don't consider vulnerability and courage as poles apart; they can be seen as two sides of the same coin.

Role in Nurturing Relationships:

The "Selfcation" approach in relationships entails a holistic perspective that considers the interconnectedness of various aspects of your life. Embrace yourself thoroughly and don't leave any part of your existence unexplored. You are a whole, more than the sum of pieces of your life. This forms a bedrock to prepare yourself to live a satisfying life in your relationships and connections.

Impact on Connections:

Adopting the "Selfcation" mindset can enhance connections within these relationships. This implies that the approach is not passive but actively contributes to making interactions and relationships more meaningful and fulfilling.

Development of Authentic Self:

"Selfcation" emphasises the power of focusing, building, and maintaining your authentic self within these relationships. This implies that the "Selfcation" approach is about genuine self-expression and authenticity rather than conformity to external expectations. Stand on your ground and defend yourself to built the person you aspire to be. You are on a journey to unleash your potential and embrace life not just for the sake of existence, but because you recognise your inherent worth. You are creating a life that is truly worth living.

Having said the above-mentioned points about the "Selfcation" approach to relationships, now is the time to start practical exercises. Wait a moment. Treat yourself to a cup of tea or coffee. Bring your notebook and pen and begin.

Following practical suggestions indicate hands-on skills, an actionable approach to implementing the mindset of "Selfcation" in real life scenarios. These practical suggestions are categorised as communication skills, preparation for healthier relationships, and finally you are cordially invited to live the "Selfcation" life. First, we start with the general practical assignments as a warm-up to help you in the "Selfcation":

1. Reflect:

Begin by reflecting on your current interactions in different areas of life, yourself, family, friends, and professional relationships. Identify situations where you feel there is room for improvement in adopting a "Selfcation" approach. Consider self-monitoring.

2. Set Realistic Goals:

Set specific and realistic goals for incorporating the "Selfcation" mindset. For example, aim to express your authentic thoughts and feelings more openly in your family conversations or actively listen and acknowledge your colleagues' perspectives in professional meetings. Once you did them, reflect on them. By practicing this, it seems you are auditing yourself in the "Selfcation" journey.

3. Daily Practice:

Create a daily practice routine. This could include setting aside a few minutes each day to consciously focus on being present in your interactions, understanding others' perspectives, and expressing your authentic self. Again auditing. Ponder here. Was it realistic? Reflect on it.

4. Track Your Progress:

Keep a journal to track your progress. Note instances where you successfully applied the "Selfcation" approach, as well as situations that presented challenges. Reflect on what you learned from each experience.

Auditing again. Is your progress on going? Is it implemented in your daily life? Is it realistic? Reflect on it. Be patient. You need to be liable and committed more at the beginning of your journey to make the "Selfcation" mindset and lifestyle as your routine.

Below there are more assignments for the communication skills, preparation for healthier relationships, and keeping you on track in the "Selfcation" journey.

1. Communication Skills:

Empathetic Listening Challenge in the following tasks:

Choose a Conversation: Identify a significant conversation you anticipate having in the near future, whether it's with a family member, friend, or colleague.

Active Listening: Focus on active listening during this conversation. Practice paraphrasing and summarising the speaker's points to ensure you truly understand the speaker's perspective.

Ask Open-Ended Questions: Challenge yourself to ask open-ended questions that encourage the other person to share more about your thoughts and feelings.

82

This fosters a deeper connection and demonstrates your commitment to understanding them.

Non-Verbal Communication: Pay attention to your non-verbal cues. Maintain eye contact, use affirmative gestures, and ensure your body language reflects openness and receptiveness.

Reflect and Learn: After the conversation, take some time to reflect on your communication skills. What went well? What could improve? Use this reflection to refine your approach in future interactions.

2. Preparation for Healthier Relationships:

The Relationship Health Audit that you can implement it in the following manner:

Identify Key Relationships: List the key relationships in your personal and professional life. This may include all kinds of relationships we discussed.

Evaluate Current Dynamics: Assess the current dynamics of each relationship. Identify aspects that contribute constructively to the relationship and areas that may need improvement.

Set Relationship Goals: Establish specific and realistic goals for each relationship. These goals should align with the principles of the "Selfcation" approach, focusing on authenticity, empathy, and effective communication.

Implement Changes: Take proactive steps to implement changes in your behaviour and communication based on the goals you set. This might involve initiating open conversations, expressing your needs, or actively listening to others.

Regular Check-Ins: Schedule regular check-ins with yourself to evaluate progress. Adjust your approach as needed and celebrate small victories in nurturing healthier relationships.

3. Invitation to the "Selfcation" Journey:

Personal Manifesto in your "Selfcation" that echoes yourself solely. You can benefit from the below sequence:

Define Your Values: Reflect on your personal values and how they align with the "Selfcation" approach. Consider aspects such as authenticity, empathy, and connection.

Write Your Manifesto: Craft a personal manifesto that outlines your commitment to the "Selfcation" journey. Describe the principles you aim to embody and the positive impact you hope to achieve in your life and relationships.

Visual Representation: Create a visual representation of your manifesto. This could be a poster, a digital graphic, or any other form that resonates with you. Display it in a prominent place as a daily reminder.

Share Your Manifesto: If you feel comfortable, share your manifesto with a close friend or family member. Discuss your intentions and invite them to join you on the "Selfcation" journey.

Reflect and Adjust: Periodically revisit your manifesto, reflect on your journey, and make adjustments as needed. This ongoing process will help you stay committed and continue evolving in your personal growth in improving the "Selfcation" mindset.

These assignments are designed to be practical, actionable, and reflective, encouraging you actively to apply the "Selfcation" approach in your daily life and relationships. Please make sure you're well-versed in the exercises of this chapter because this chapter provide a platform to build yourself in the "Selfcation" journey. You will add to this "Selfcation" booklet in the coming chapters.

In summary, this chapter encourages you to embrace the "Selfcation" approach, offering understanding and practical guidance for applying this mindset to enhance various aspects of your life and relationships. In the coming section, self-care and wellness importance will be discussed.

Life keeps moving on, and yet remains profoundly rooted in the present, seeking no result, for the present has spread out from its constriction in an elusive pin-point of strained consciousness to an all-embracing eternity. Feelings both positive and negative come and go without turmoil, for they seem to be simply observed, though there is no one observing. They pass trackless like birds in the sky, and build up no resistances which have to be dissipated in reckless action.

Alan W. Watts

6. Self-Care and Wellness

Self-care and wellness are interconnected concepts that focus on promoting and maintaining your physical, mental, emotional, social, and spiritual well-being. They involve intentional actions and practices that contribute to a healthy and balanced lifestyle. Take a deep breath. Have your notebook and pen ready. Here's an overview of both concepts:

Self-care and wellness go beyond the absence of illness and emphasises a proactive approach to health. They refer to the deliberate activities and practices you engage in to maintain your physical, mental, emotional, social, and spiritual health. It involves recognising your needs and taking proactive steps to meet those needs. The components of self-care can be practiced as follow:

1.   Physical Self-Care:

This includes activities that support physical health, such as regular exercise, proper nutrition, adequate sleep, and hygiene practices.

If physical activities are not included in your current routine, start with baby steps. We mentioned earlier that you need to set realistic goals, so begin with achievable objectives. No matter how small they may seem, just take that first step.

If you are already engaging in physical activities, take a moment to reflect on your current plan and audit it for potential improvements.

2.   Mental Self-Care:

Mental well-being involves activities that stimulate and challenge the mind. This can include reading, learning new skills, problem-solving, and engaging in creative pursuits. Also, meditation is a part of mental self-care. Focus or cognitive health, emotional resilience, stress management, and intellectua stimulation.

If you've reached here, kudos to you. Now you have good knowledge abou yourself and you know your limits. In the mental self-care, basically, challenge yourself and soothe yourself. By doing so, you're stretching your comfor zone.

3. Emotional Self-Care:

Encompasses self-awareness, emotional regulation, and the ability to navigate and cope with life's ups and downs. Improving emotional well-being encompasses a variety of practices, including mindfulness to stay present, journaling for self-reflection, seeking the support from those close to you, and engaging in activities that bring both joy and relaxation into your daily life. Don't keep everything inside. Open up and put them in words or any visual realisation.

4. Social Self-Care:

Building and maintaining constructive relationships contribute to social well-being. This involves spending quality me-time as well as quality time with others, nurturing connections, and setting healthy boundaries.

5. Spiritual Self-Care:

For those with spiritual inclinations, practices like meditation, prayer, or spending time in nature can contribute to a sense of purpose and connection with the superpower as well as nature. This dimension involves connecting with one's values, purpose, and a sense of transcendence.

Having said that, you can help yourself to be committed and liable to your self-care and wellness practices by emphasising the important to adhere to them that are discussed in the following part. Importance of self-care and wellness can be traced in preventing health action, enhancing resilience, and enhancing mental health.

Preventative Health Actions: Regular self-care and wellness help prevention in different levels, i.e. primary prevention, secondary prevention, and tertiary prevention. The preventions can be continued, but we stop here to be manageable for you in action. By practicing self-care and wellness practices, you can tackle any potential triggers to prevent and take action before they burst.

Enhances Resilience: Those who prioritise self-care are often better equipped to cope with life's challenges and setbacks. By practicing self-care, you empower yourself to take an active role in your life, enhancing your sense of agency. This increased agency enables you to make informed decisions and better navigate life's uncertainties, ultimately improving your overall life management.

Improves Mental Health: Self-care practices can contribute to improved mental health outcomes, including reduced anxiety and depression. Implementing self-care practices in your daily life, support having meaningful life. Once the meaning is there, all your life will be to obtain the meaning. We discussed the meaning in chapter 7. You can refer to it and reflect based on the knowledge you've gained so far.

You nailed it by reaching here. Hats off to you. Treat yourself to a delicious snack and then hit the road again.

Are you back? You deserve a pat on the back.

In summary, self-care and wellness are intertwined concepts that underscore the importance of intentional actions and habits in nurturing a balanced and fulfilling life. They involve a proactive commitment to your health and well-being, recognising the interconnectedness of various aspects of life. In the coming chapters of this section prioritising self-case and well-being, nurturing physical and mental health, and finally managing stress and finding balance will be discussed.

Chapter 13

Prioritising Self-Care and Well-Being

This chapter emphasises the importance of self-care and well-being in achieving a balanced and satisfying life. Also, it serves as a foundation for self-care and wellness. It underscores the importance of prioritising your well-being in the hectic pace of life. As the foundation upon which a harmonious existence is built, the importance of prioritising your well-being is underscored, offering you a compass for navigating the complexities of a fast-paced life. You will learn practical strategies for prioritising your physical and mental health, including establishing self-care routines and setting boundaries. We follow this route in five sections namely the essence of self-care, prioritising well-being in a busy world, strategies for physical and mental health, establishing self-care routines, and setting and maintaining boundaries. They are stated as below:

Section 1: The Essence of Self-Care

We touched upon the self-care recently. Here we go through it deeper by begining unraveling the essence of self-care, shedding light on why it is more than just a trendy buzzword. Exploring the intrinsic link between self-care and well-being, we lay the groundwork for understanding how intentional and compassionate practices contribute to a more satisfying life. We're taking a hands-on approach to demystify self-care, moving beyond its popular buzzword status. Let's break down what we mean by exploring the essence of self-care practically:

1. Going Beyond Trends:

Trace the roots of self-care by reflecting on its historical context. Consider how societies and cultures throughout time have embraced self-care practices.

Engage in a brief exercise where you identify self-care practices from different historical periods and cultures, recognising the enduring nature of these practices, e.g., discover the practice of Japanese forest bathing (shinrin-yoku) and incorporate a nature walk into your routine, connecting with the timeless tradition of immersing oneself in the healing power of nature.

2. Intrinsic Connection with Well-Being:

Reflect on moments in your life when you genuinely took care of yourself and felt a positive impact on your overall well-being.

Consider creating a visual representation or journal entry that illustrates the connections between specific self-care activities and your well-being.

3. Intentional and Compassionate Practices:

List activities that bring you joy, relaxation, and a sense of peace. You may have this list. If yes, review and administer the current task.

Select one activity from your list and schedule time for it intentionally in your upcoming week. Observe how the intentional act of setting aside time for self-care impacts your experience.

4. Contributions to Fulfillment:

Identify areas of your life where you feel unfulfilled or stressed.

Integrate a self-care practice into those areas and observe how it contributes to a greater sense of fulfillment. This could be as simple as taking short breaks during work or dedicating time to pursue a hobby. Reflect on the steps you take.

5. Empowering Yourself:

Create a list of self-care practices that resonate with you personally.

Choose one practice from your list to incorporate into your daily or weekly routine. Reflect on how this intentional practice empowers you and positively influences your overall well-being.

These practical assignments allow you to actively engage with the essence of self-care in the "Selfcation" journey. By incorporating intentional and compassionate practices into your life, you move beyond theoretical concepts and observe the tangible impact of self-care on your well-being.

Section 2: Prioritising Well-Being in a Busy World

The relentless pace of modern life emphasises the critical need to prioritise well-being. By acknowledging the challenges posed by a hectic lifestyle, you are guided through the importance of carving out dedicated time for self-care

Practical insights are provided to help you weave moments of well-being into your daily routines.

1. Acknowledging the Challenges:

Identify specific challenges in your daily life that hinder well-being.

Recognise factors such as long work hours, digital distractions, or a demanding tight schedule. Acknowledge these challenges without judgement, understanding that many individuals face similar obstacles. You are not alone and you can find a way to streamline your self-care, and well-being no matter how challenging such obstacles are.

2. Carving Out Dedicated Time:

Evaluate your daily schedule for potential time slots to accommodate self-care and well-being activities. Plan a daily well-being routine.

Review your typical day and identify pockets of time that can be allocated to well-being. This could include a 15-minute break during work, an early morning routine, or moments before bedtime. Acknowledge that small, intentional time blocks can make a significant impact.

Structure your day to include moments of well-being seamlessly. For instance, if mornings are less hectic, allocate time for mindfulness or a healthy breakfast. Build these routines gradually, adapting them to suit your lifestyle and preferences.

3. Weaving Moments of Well-Being:

List specific well-being activities that resonate with you.

Choose one activity, such as meditation or a brief walk, that aligns with your preferences. Integrate this activity into your schedule during the identified time slots. Consistency is key; make a commitment to weave these moments into your daily routine.

4. Practical Insights:

Reflect on potential barriers to consistency.

Anticipate challenges that might arise, such as work deadlines or unexpected commitments. Develop practical strategies to overcome these barriers, such as setting reminders, creating a dedicated space for well-being activities, or involving a friend for mutual accountability.

5. Reflecting on Impact:

Journal about your experiences.

Keep a well-being journal to document your well-being in the "Selfcation" journey. Note how these intentional moments impact your mood, energy levels, and overall satisfaction. Reflect on the constructive changes you observe, reinforcing the importance of prioritising well-being. To support the well-being in tangible way, body image is introduced here.

All of us have image from ourselves in our mind. It is referred to body image specifically. Body-image refers to an individuals' perceptions, thoughts, and feelings about their own body. It involves how one sees their body in terms of size, shape, weight, and overall appearance. Body image can be influenced by societal standards, cultural factors, media representation, personal experiences, and mental health. Positive body image entails a healthy and realistic view of one's body, while negative body image involves dissatisfaction or distorted perceptions, which can contribute to mental health issues such as eating disorders and low self-compassion and positive affirmation.

You can draw your body image on a paper and keep it with you. Revisit this image time to time and draw another one once you feel the time has come for change in your body image. Intentionally reflect your drawing. Try to make as realistic as possible and give yourself positive affirmation.

Please note body image is different than self-image and self-concept. They are related concepts, but they are different than each other. I mention these concepts in case you want to explore more to improve your self-development

6. Creating Well-Being Reminders:

Set visual reminders.

Use visual cues like sticky notes or phone alerts to prompt well-being activities. These reminders serve as gentle nudges, helping you stay committed to prioritising well-being amidst the busyness.

This practical approach encourages you to actively engage with the challenges of a busy life and intentionally carve out moments for well-being.

By acknowledging, planning, and reflecting, you can gradually accommodate the essence of well-being into your daily routines.

Section 3: Strategies for Physical and Mental Health

Such strategies serve as practical toolkit, offering you actionable ways for prioritising both physical and mental health. From establishing self-care routines that align with your lifestyles to setting and maintaining healthy boundaries, each strategy is carefully crafted to empower you on your well-being journey in the "Selfcation".

1. Establishing a Fitness Schedule:

Set realistic fitness targets.

Determine the frequency and duration of your physical activities. Create a weekly fitness schedule, incorporating both cardiovascular exercises and strength training to address comprehensive well-being.

2. Prioritising Sleep Hygiene:

Sleep hygiene refers to a set of practices and habits that promote good sleep quality and overall sleep health. It involves creating a conducive sleep environment and adopting routines that support consistent and restful sleep.

Key aspects of sleep hygiene include maintaining a regular sleep schedule, creating a relaxing bedtime routine, optimising the sleep environment, and avoiding factors that can disrupt sleep, such as excessive screen time before bedtime or stimulants like caffeine. Adopting good sleep hygiene practices contributes to better overall well-being and helps preventing sleep disturbances.

Identify areas for improvement in your sleep routine, such as maintaining a consistent sleep schedule, creating a calming bedtime routine, and optimising your sleep environment.

Assess your current sleep habits.

3. Incorporating Mindfulness Practices:

Experiment with mindfulness techniques.

Try mindfulness meditation or deep-breathing exercises that we discussed before. Integrate these practices into your daily routine, such as a short mindfulness session during breaks or before bedtime.

4. Creating a Balanced Work-Life Integration:

Assess your work-life balance.

Establish boundaries between work and personal time. Schedule breaks, plan leisure activities, and communicate clearly with colleagues about your designated non-work hours.

5. Engaging in Stress-Relief Activities:

List activities that alleviate stress.

Choose stress-relief activities like reading, listening to music, or spending time in nature. Regularly incorporate these activities into your routine to manage stress proactively.

6. Tracking Progress and Adjusting Strategies:

Keep a well-being journal.

Regularly assess your progress toward physical and mental health goals. Note any adjustments needed to your strategies based on your experiences and evolving well-being needs. Self-monitoring is an ongoing process that you need to keep an eye on it.

7. Seeking Professional Support:

Search local well-being resources.

Identify professionals or support groups that align with your well-being goals. Consider reaching out for expert guidance when needed, recognise the value of seeking support in your journey.

This hands-on toolkit provides you with effective strategies, empowering you to assume control over both your physical and mental well-being. By customising these strategies to fit your unique lifestyle and needs, you embark on a well-being journey that is both intentional and sustainable in the

"Selfcation" lifestyle. You are building up your personal guidance, the booklet that for you to unlock your potential.

Subsection 4: Establishing Self-Care Routines

Delving into the significance of consistent self-care practices provides concrete steps and examples to guide you in creating routines that cater to your unique needs, from morning rituals to evening wind-downs, discover how intentional habits can transform your daily experience. By delving into the significance of these routines, it aims to provide practical guidance and examples, offering a roadmap for creating habits that align with your individual needs. Here's a breakdown:

1.   Significance of Consistency:

Recognising that self-care is not just an occasional indulgence but a fundamental aspect of overall well-being. Consistent practices contribute to the sustained nourishment of your physical, mental, and emotional health.

2.   Concrete Steps:

Offering tangible, actionable steps to help yourself establish self-care routines. This might include specific activities, timeframes, and considerations for incorporating self-care seamlessly into your daily life.

3.   Guidance for Unique Needs:

Acknowledge the diversity of your needs and preferences. You need to tailor self-care routines to suit your unique circumstances, take into account factors such as personal interests, and daily schedules.

4.   Morning Rituals to Evening Wind-Downs:

Exploring the full spectrum of the day, from morning rituals that set a positive tone for the day to evening wind-downs that facilitate relaxation and restful sleep. This comprehensive approach ensures that self-care is integrated into every aspect of daily living.

Some people function better during the day, referred to as morning larks, while others thrive at night, namely night owls. Regardless of whether you are a day or night person, it's essential to incorporate self-care practices throughout your entire day.

5. Intentional Habits and Transformation:

Emphasising the transformative power of intentional habits. By being deliberate and mindful in the practice of self-care, you can experience a positive shift in your daily experiences, improving a sense of balance, satisfaction, and overall well-being.

The body image that you draw in the previous section, now draw another body image drawing that you want to have in future. Please note body image is not only about body, it is more about the perception that you have about your body, thoughts, etc. that mentioned before.

Basically, this section serves as a practical guide, encouraging you to view self-care not as a sporadic event but as a consistent and intentional practice. Through concrete steps, relatable examples, and personalised guidance, it aims to empower you to create self-care routines that become integral parts of your daily lives, contributing to a wholistic and transformative well-being journey.

Subsection 5: Setting and Maintaining Boundaries

Setting boundaries is a vital factor in the "Selfcation" journey that has been explored from the beginning of this book. Recognising the importance of healthy boundaries in preserving well-being explores the art of setting limits without guilt. Practical tips are presented to help you navigate the delicate balance between giving to others and preserving energy for your self-care in the "Selfcation" lifestyle.

1. Preserving Well-Being without Guilt:

Emphasising the art of establishing boundaries without succumbing to feelings of guilt. This aspect is crucial as many individuals may find it challenging to set limits due to societal expectations or personal obligations.

Think what you would do in the absence of outside pressure. Do it now. It helps you to protect your well-being.

2. Practical Tips for Boundary-Setting:

Providing actionable advice and tips for setting effective boundaries may include communication strategies, assertiveness techniques, and ways to clearly define personal limits in various areas of life that were covered in the previous chapters.

3.   Navigating the Balance between Giving and Self-Care:

Addressing the delicate balance between providing support to others and ensuring adequate energy is preserved for self-care. Setting boundaries doesn't necessarily mean being selfish as we discuss at the beginning of the book. It is a vital component of maintaining your ability to give and contribute effectively in real life.

By exploring the delicate dance of setting and maintaining boundaries, this section aims to empower you with practical tools for navigating relationships, work, and personal commitments while safeguarding your well-being. The ultimate goal is to foster a sense of agency and confidence in you, allowing you to establish boundaries with purpose and compassion for both yourself and others.

As this chapter concludes, you are equipped with a robust understanding of self-care and well-being as indispensable components of a balanced and fulfilling life. The practical strategies shared serve as actionable tools, empowering you to embark on a journey toward sustained well-being amid life's demands. Nurturing physical and mental health will be explored in the coming chapter.

Chapter 14

Nurturing Physical and Mental Health

T his chapter searches deeper into the specifics of physical and mental well-being. There is an intricate link between your physical and mental well-being. You will gain insights into nurturing your holistic wellness. You will explore the connection between your physical well-being (nutrition, exercise, sleep) and your mental health (stress management, mindfulness, emotional well-being). Practical suggestions, exercises, and resources will guide you on the "Selfcation" journey to a healthier, and happier self. Here are examples of what you can practice:

1. Nurturing Physical Well-Being:

Delve into practical advice on optimising your physical health. Learn about nutrition choices that fuel your body, effective exercise routines tailored to your lifestyle, and strategies for ensuring restful sleep. These insights form the foundation for a healthier and more energised you.

Engage in a mind-body connection exercise, such as yoga or tai chi. Explore how these practices impact both your physical and mental well-being. Document your experience, noting any changes in mood, energy levels, or physical sensations.

2. Cultivating Mental Resilience:

Explore techniques for managing stress, more about stress management will be provided in the next chapter, incorporating mindfulness into your daily routine, and improving emotional well-being. Practical exercises will empower you to build mental resilience and equip you with tools to navigate life's challenges with a positive mindset.

3. Curated Resources for Continuous Growth:

Access a curated collection of resources to support your well-being journey. They could be readings, online courses, or wellness apps, these resources are designed to empower you in your pursuit of a healthier, happier self.

Embark on this practical journey toward holistic well-being. By implementing the advice, engaging in exercises, and utilising resources, you'll not only understand the dynamics of physical and mental health but also take tangible steps toward cultivating a more balanced and fulfilling life.

These practical assignments are designed to encourage active engagement with the principles discussed in this chapter. By actively completing these assignments, you're not only enhance your understanding of holistic well-being but also embark on tangible actions to improve a healthier and more balanced lifestyle.

More insight and information will be shared about stress management and finding balance in the coming chapter.

Chapter 15

Managing Stress and Finding Balance

L ife in the 21st century often comes with its own set of challenges. Juggling multiple responsibilities and navigating a fast-paced world can take a toll on our well-being. In this chapter, we delve into stress management, its critical aspects, and finding balance in life's demands. Stress is an inseparable part of our lives.

It is worth mentioning two kinds of stress, i.e., distress and eustress, and differentiate them. These are terms used in psychology to describe different types of stress in terms of their function in daily life. While both involve a state of mental or emotional strain, they represent opposite ends of the stress spectrum in terms of their impact on well-being. Also, they have different functions.

Distress refers to negative or destructive stress, often characterised by feelings of discomfort, anxiety, and strain. It is the type of stress that is typically harmful and can have adverse effects on both mental and physical health.

Distress can be caused by various factors, including challenging life events, chronic difficulties, trauma, and situations that exceed an individual's coping abilities.

Symptoms of distress may include increased heart rate, muscle tension, fatigue, irritability, difficulty concentrating, and a range of emotional responses such as sadness or anxiety.

Prolonged exposure to distress can lead to health problems such as cardiovascular issues, weakened immune function, and mental health disorders like anxiety and depression.

Eustress, on the other hand, is positive or constructive stress, characterised by feelings of excitement, motivation, and fulfillment. Unlike distress, eustress is seen as beneficial and can enhance performance and well-being.

Eustress is often associated with situations that are challenging but manageable, such as starting a new job, pursuing a personal goal, or engaging in an enjoyable activity.

While eustress may still activate the body's stress response, the accompanying feelings are more positive. Eustress can lead to increased focus, heightened energy levels, and a sense of accomplishment.

Eustress can serve as a motivating force, prompting you to overcome challenges, set and achieve goals, and experience a sense of accomplishment and personal growth.

In certain situations, eustress can enhance cognitive performance and creativity. It is associated with the optimal level of alertness that promotes peak performance without causing negative consequences.

Understanding the distinction between distress and eustress is crucial for managing stress effectively. While distress requires attention and coping strategies to alleviate its destructive impact, eustress represents a healthy and constructive form of stress that can contribute to personal growth and fulfillment. Striking a balance between the two is essential in your "Selfcation" journey for maintaining overall well-being and constructively navigating life's challenges.

You feel stress when a stressor, anything that causes you stress or tension, triggers your body's stress response, releasing stress hormones like adrenaline and cortisol. The definition of a stressor varies from person to person: For example, public speaking may be a stressor for some people and a joy for others. Common types of stressors include:

Routine stressors: Everyday stress is an integral aspect of our lives. Whether it's preparing dinner, navigating through traffic, managing work or school responsibilities, tidying up the house, or attending to the needs of family and friends, these activities collectively contribute to a pervasive undercurrent of daily stress.

Disruptive stressors: Disruptive stress has the power to interrupt our daily routines, commanding our immediate attention. Events such as sudden illness or injury, a divorce or breakup, financial troubles like bankruptcy, and the loss of employment fall into the category of disruptive stressors. The impact of these stressors may escalate to the level of traumatic stress, influenced by our individual experiences of these events.

Traumatic stressors: Trauma represents an emotional reaction to an intensely high-stress, or perilous event, relationship, or situation that poses a threat to our well-being or safety. Instances giving rise to traumatic stress encompass war, assault, abuse, natural disasters, terrorism, and serious accidents.

In the short term, your body's stress response is a natural and beneficial reaction. It aids in maintaining wakefulness and alertness, focusing your attention, sustaining motivation, avoiding immediate dangers, responding to threats, and prioritising your safety and survival.

However, when these short-term reactions persist as long-term symptoms, stress may adversely affect both your mental and physical health. Understanding how stress manifests in your life and recognising its sources is a key aspect of self-awareness. This knowledge empowers you to implement effective stress management strategies, leading to improved mental and emotional well-being.

Now we know there are constructive stress and destructive stress and it is important to differentiate them. In addition, it's useful to expand your knowledge about stress in terms of the duration it lasts as well, e.g. acute stress and chronic stress. Take a deep breath and then continue.

Acute stress vs. chronic stress: Acute stress is a widespread experience, with everyone encountering it. It manifests in response to sudden changes or perceived threats. Situations inducing acute stress need not be prolonged; they can be brief, such as the intense studying leading to a final exam.

In contrast, chronic stress arises from enduring or persistent stressors that extend over weeks or months. Financial predicaments, and break up are examples of circumstances that can lead to chronic stress.

Quickly we review stress disorders as per The Diagnostic and Statistical Manual of Mental Disorders (DSM) 5. This reference is used by experts in diagnosis. Here we review just to make yourself familiar with these academic terms. Stress disorders are mental health disorders that may develop after you go through or witness trauma. Common types include:

Acute stress disorder (ASD), whose symptoms persist for less than a month after the trauma occurred. ASD symptoms include anxiety, dissociation or feeling disconnected from reality, and avoiding situations that remind a person of the trauma.

Posttraumatic stress disorder (PTSD), whose symptoms persist for more than a month after the trauma occurred. PTSD symptoms include intrusive memories, thinking and mood changes, and hypervigilance or extreme alertness to threats.

It is good to know stress can contribute to, worsen, or be a symptom of other mental health disorders including, but not limited to anxiety, depression, obsessive-compulsive disorder, insomnia, and drug misuse or Addiction. Treat yourself to a cup of tea or coffee. Hope you're not stressed by reading about stress. In the coming part approaches in stress coping strategies will be defined.

In a wide scope, there are two distinct approaches to dealing with stress namely, person-oriented coping and problem-oriented coping. These coping strategies focus on different aspects of the stress experience and involve unique methods for managing and adapting to stressors.

Person-oriented coping centers on managing the emotional and psychological impact of stress by addressing one's own emotional reactions and well-being. It emphasises emotional regulation and self-awareness. In person-oriented oping focuses on understanding and managing your feelings and thoughts in response to stress. Also, it involves seeking emotional support from others or engaging in activities that promote emotional well-being. For example, after receiving negative feedback at work, a person-oriented coping strategy might involve reflecting on personal feelings, seeking comfort from friends or family, and engaging in activities that bring emotional relief, such as practicing mindfulness or engaging in hobbies.

Problem-oriented coping involves taking practical steps to address and solve the specific problems or stressors causing stress. To implement this kind of coping strategy, focuses on identifying and resolving the root causes of stress. It involves problem-solving, planning, and taking direct action to change or manage the situation. Also, it aims to enhance your sense of control by actively addressing stressors. For example, if a student is feeling overwhelmed by academic demands, a problem-oriented coping strategy might include creating a detailed study schedule, seeking additional resources or tutoring, and breaking down complex tasks into smaller, more manageable steps.

It can be concluded that person-oriented coping, primarily centers on managing emotional reactions and well-being, involves emotional regulation, self-reflection, and seeking emotional support, and is often used when the stressor is not easily controllable or changeable, so it focuses on adapting emotionally to the situation.

Problem-oriented coping centers on identifying and addressing the root causes of stress, involves problem-solving, planning, and taking direct action to change the situation, and it is applicable when there are specific actions that can be taken to address and resolve the stressor.

In practice, you may use a combination of both person-oriented and problem-oriented coping strategies based on the nature of the stressor and your personal preferences. The effectiveness of these strategies can vary depending on the context and your overall coping repertoire.

Besides person-oriented and problem-oriented coping, researchers and psychologists have identified several other coping strategies that individuals may apply in response to stress. Below are suggestions for stress copying practices by implementing these coping styles.

1. Emotion-Focused Coping:

This strategy involves managing emotional responses to stress without necessarily addressing the root cause. Individuals using emotion-focused coping may engage in activities that soothe or distract from emotional distress. Listening to music, practicing relaxation techniques, or engaging in activities that bring comfort are suggestions in benefitting from emotion-focused coping

2. Avoidant Coping:

Avoidant coping involves efforts to escape or avoid stressors altogether. It can include denial, distraction, or disengagement from the stressful situation Ignoring a problem, avoiding conflict, or engaging in activities to divert attention from the stressor are examples of avoiding coping practices.

3. Humour Coping:

Humour coping involves using humour and laughter to alleviate stress and lighten the mood. It can be an effective way to reframe situations and reduce tension. Finding humour in a challenging situation, telling jokes, or watching a funny movie to shift one's perspective are examples of humour coping.

4. Spiritual Coping:

Drawing on spiritual beliefs to find meaning, comfort, or guidance during stressful times. It often involves prayer, meditation, or participation in spiritual rituals.

5. Proactive Coping:

This strategy involves taking preventive measures to manage potential stressors before they become overwhelming. It emphasises anticipation and planning. Proactively managing time, setting realistic goals, and implementing stress-reducing activities in anticipation of future challenges are tasks you can benefit from.

Rather than the coping strategies mentioned, there are some techniques you can benefit from in stress management. Below common practices to manage stress are suggested:

1. Mindfulness and Relaxation Techniques:

Introducing mindfulness practices, such as deep breathing, meditation, and progressive muscle relaxation, empowers you to cultivate a heightened awareness of the present moment. These techniques serve as powerful tools for reducing stress and promoting mental well-being. Mostly, they slow down the physical symptoms to manage stress.

2. Cognitive Behavioural Techniques:

Cognitive restructuring entails the practice of recognising and challenging negative thought patterns. The goal is to identify and change distorted thinking, ultimately transforming how you perceive and respond to stressors. By actively engaging in this process, you can cultivate a more balanced and constructive perspective, leading to healthier emotional and behavioural responses in the face of stress. You navigate your emotions and thoughts to nail down the stress.

To recap we talked about stress management and finding balance in this chapter. By understanding the foundations of stress, implementing effective coping strategies, and embracing the concept of balance, you can navigate life's challenges with greater resilience and well-being. The key lies in the consistent application of these principles, turning them into enduring habits for a healthier and more balanced life in your "Selfcation" journey.

Now is the time to talk about financial and career empowerment in the "Selfcation" journey. Ponder here and review your notes and responses. Refresh your mind and then start the next section.

Even a correct decision is wrong when it is taken too late.

Lee Iacocca

7. Financial and Career Empowerment:

Financial and career empowerment represents a transformative journey towards achieving self-sufficiency, stability, and satisfaction in both financial and professional spheres. It encapsulates a holistic approach to personal development, encompassing strategies and practices that enable you to take control of your financial well-being and career trajectories in the "Selfcation" lifestyle.

This empowerment process involves acquiring essential financial literacy skills, cultivating a proactive mindset, and making informed decisions that align with long-term goals. By merging financial prudence with strategic career planning, you can pave the way for increased financial security, expanded opportunities, and a more resilient and rewarding professional life. In the coming chapters, financial health and wealth building, and career development and achieving success will be discussed. Finally, the "Selfcation" approach to finances and career development will be presented.

Chapter 16

Financial Health and Wealth Building

In this chapter, we focus on the cornerstone of a stable and prosperous life through financial empowerment. We will explore the foundations of financial health, including budgeting, saving, and investing. This chapter delves into strategies for building wealth and securing your financial future. It provides practical suggestions, tips, and tools to help you improve your financial well-being, understand money management, and work towards your financial goals.

Before starting off the chapter, it is better to start listing your current resources that can help you in your financial endeavour. Even if you do not work currently, start writing about your abilities, skills, and experiences. Then, search for demanding fields, find any potential overlap between them, and explore opportunities in those areas. By having this list in hand, you streamline your roadmap for pursuing financial attempts and career goals.

Foundations of Financial Health:

Understanding the fundamentals of financial health is the first step toward empowerment. We explore the art of budgeting, teaching you how to allocate your resources wisely, prioritise spending, and create a financial roadmap tailored to your unique goals. Through insightful discussions, you will gain a comprehensive grasp of the role budgeting plays in achieving long-term financial stability.

Budgeting is the cornerstone of financial success. You need to be well-rounded in the process of creating a budget tailored to your income, expenses, and financial goals. You need to allocate funds effectively, prioritise spending based on your values, and develop a sustainable budget that aligns with your lifestyle.

Understanding the importance of tracking expenses, distinguishing between two things, needs and wants, expenses and investments, and making informed decisions about discretionary spending are key components covered that you need to observe constantly. The goal is to empower you to take control of your financial life through conscious and intentional budgeting. Bring your notebook and pen.

Start by tracking your monthly income and expenses. Create a budget that allocates specific amounts to necessities, savings, and discretionary spending.

Use budgeting apps or spreadsheets to categorise expenses. Regularly review and adjust your budget based on your financial goals and changing circumstances. Reflect on your budging plan.

After budgeting, we move on to saving. Saving is not just a habit; it's a powerful tool for securing your financial well-being. This part equips you with practical tips on how to cultivate a saving mindset, set achievable saving goals, and build an emergency fund. Whether you're planning for short-term goals or creating a safety net for unexpected expenses, you need to make saving an integral part of your financial strategy.

Saving is not just about setting money aside; it's a part of "Selfcation" mindset. You should consider the psychological aspects of saving, helping you understand the importance of delayed gratification and the long-term benefits of consistent saving habits. You'll gain insights into overcoming common barriers to saving and developing a positive relationship with money. Prior to the practical application and the implementation step, you find information about the psychological aspects of saving, specifically Behavioural Economics.

Behavioural Economics is a field of study that combines insights from psychology and economics to understand how individuals make decisions and choices, especially in situations involving uncertainty or ambiguity. Unlike traditional economic models that assume people always make rational decisions to maximise their utility or well-being, behavioural economics acknowledges that individuals often deviate from purely rational behaviour due to cognitive biases and emotional factors. Here are two behavioural biases that have huge impacts along with suggestions to overcome them:

1. Loss Aversion:

Loss aversion is the tendency for individuals to prefer avoiding losses over acquiring equivalent gains. In other words, the pain of losing something is psychologically more significant than the pleasure of gaining the same thing.

Loss aversion can impact saving behaviour by making individuals more risk-averse. They might be reluctant to take actions that could result in potential losses, even if those actions have the potential for greater long-term gains. This aversion to losses can lead to conservative investment choices or resistance to changes in financial strategies.

To overcome it, take small steps to address loss aversion. Reflect on a situation in which you experienced loss, consider the lessons learnt, and try to embrace the feelings associated with loss aversion. Immerse yourself deeply in these emotions, and seek to find an alternative narrative for this loss. Examine the justifications you bring up. After that, attempt to observe the situation from a distance, as if it were happening to another person. What suggestions would you offer to this person? Apply those suggestions in your life.

2. Present Bias:

Present bias refers to the tendency of individuals to prioritise immediate rewards over larger, but delayed, rewards. People often prefer instant gratification and may struggle to make choices that benefit them in the long term. Present bias can negatively impact saving behaviour by leading individuals to prioritise immediate consumption over saving for future needs. This bias may contribute to a lack of long-term planning and difficulty in building up savings for goals like retirement. Individuals with a present bias may find it challenging to resist spending money now in favour of saving for the future.

The first step to overcome this issue is to spare some amount of whatever funds you receive. Also, whenever you want to buy something and spend money, wait for five seconds, and then decide. You can increase these five seconds gradually. Once you are comfortable you can withhold spending and put the money aside. Check on a weekly or monthly basis how much money you save. You can reward yourself with that money.

Understanding these biases is crucial for designing effective interventions to encourage positive and constructive financial behaviours. Policymakers, financial institutions, and individuals can use this knowledge to implement strategies that mitigate the impact of these biases, such as implementing automatic savings plans, providing clear incentives, or framing choices in a way that aligns with individuals' natural tendencies. By acknowledging and addressing behavioural biases, it's possible to create more effective and realistic approaches to financial decision-making and saving. Now we continue with the practical applications and the implementation steps.

Are you there? Pat on your shoulder that you've reached here, way to go, collect yourself, and continue.

Set a saving goal, such as building an emergency fund equal to three or six months' worth of living expenses. This doesn't have any contradiction with your other goals, so you can save penny by penny and keep it aside. You accumulate your savings in this manner for this goal. You may convert the money to something else or strong currencies to protect the value of your fund.

Automatically transfer a portion of your income to a dedicated savings account. Celebrate milestones as you reach your savings targets. Here are more practices to assist you.

1. Setting Achievable Saving Goals:

Effective saving involves setting clear and achievable goals. Here is the guidance on how to identify short-term and long-term saving objectives, whether it's for an emergency fund, a major purchase, or retirement. Learn how to create a realistic saving plan that aligns with your financial aspirations.

Break down larger saving goals into smaller, achievable targets. For example, saving for a vacation or a down payment on a car can be achieved by accumulating small savings.

Set specific and measurable goals, create a timeline, and regularly assess your progress. Adjust your goals as needed.

2. Building an Emergency Fund:

An emergency fund serves as a financial safety net. From determining the right fund size to strategies for consistently contributing to it, you'll gain the tools to navigate unexpected financial challenges with confidence and peace of mind.

Establish an emergency fund to cover unexpected expenses like medical bill or car repair.

Set up a separate savings account for emergencies. Contribute a fixed amount each month until you reach your desired fund size, e.g. from all funds that you earn, keep 10% of them aside as a self-insurance. Whenever you reach a decent fund size, you can allocate some amount to other goals.

Now your knowledge is good enough to take a step forward and enter another realm in finance. We are going to dig into the art and science of investing.

Diving into the world of investing, we demystify the complexities and empower you with the knowledge needed to make informed decisions. From understanding different investment devices to assessing risk and return, you'll gain insights into crafting an investment portfolio aligned with your financial goals. This section provides practical suggestions on navigating the markets, making strategic investment choices, and harnessing the power of compound growth. We continue the practical suggestions.

3. Understanding Different Investment Devices:

Investing can be complex, but it doesn't have to be overwhelming. There are various investment options, such as stocks, bonds, mutual funds, and real estate. You should gain a comprehensive understanding of the risks and rewards associated with each, empowering you to make informed decisions based on your risk tolerance and financial goals before taking action. Risk tolerance pertains to the level of potential loss an investor is willing to endure when making an investment choice.

Assess your risk tolerance by psychometric tests. In addition, determine what kind of investor you would be, i.e., aggressive, moderate, or conservative.

Search various investment options based on your risk tolerance and financial goals.

Diversify your investments by considering a mix of stocks, bonds, and other assets as per your risk tolerance level. Don't put all your eggs in one basket. Consider consulting with a financial advisor for personalised advice. Here we just taste the waters that you get to know these concepts for more explorations.

4. Assessing Risk and Return:

Investing involves navigating the balance between risk and return. You need to have insights into risk assessment, helping yourself understand how to evaluate different investments based on your potential returns and associated risks. Generally, a thoughtful and comprehensive approach to risk and return analysis serves as the bedrock for crafting a resilient and well-balanced investment strategy.

Evaluate the risk and potential return of each investment before making decisions.

Use risk assessment tools to understand your risk tolerance. Balance high-risk, high-reward investments with more stable options for a diversified portfolio.

Reflect on yourself as well as your investments to take wiser steps in the future.

Register your steps and reflect on them to educate and equip yourself for future attempts. Now we continue by strategies for wealth building.

Building wealth is a deliberate and strategic process. here you unveil tried-and-true strategies for accumulating assets, increasing income, and maximising returns. Whether you're just starting or looking to accelerate your wealth-building journey, this chapter offers a roadmap to create lasting financial prosperity. Fasten your seatbelt and continue.

5.   Accumulating Assets:

Building wealth involves accumulating assets over time. You need to explore strategies for increasing your net worth, including strategies for debt management, increasing income streams, and leveraging assets effectively. You discover practical steps to grow your wealth and create a solid financial foundation gradually.

Develop strategies to increase your income, such as negotiating a salary raise or starting a side hustle.

Identify opportunities for career advancement, skill development, or additional income streams. Strategically manage debts to avoid hindering wealth accumulation.

6.   Maximising Returns:

Making your money work for you is a key aspect of wealth building. There are strategies for maximising investment returns, including the power of compounding and the importance of long-term thinking. Learn how to optimise your investment portfolio to achieve sustainable and consistent returns over time.

Leverage the power of compounding by starting to invest early and consistently.

Set up automatic contributions to your investment accounts. Reinvest dividends to accelerate wealth growth over time. One more step. You need to think ahead and secure your financial future as much as possible.

The ultimate goal of financial empowerment is to secure a prosperous future. You need to be equipped by tools to assess your current financial standing, set realistic milestones, and develop a roadmap for the years ahead. Also, explore strategies for retirement planning. Long-term financial security, ensuring that you have the knowledge and confidence to shape a financially resilient future.

7. Assessing Your Financial Standing:

To plan for the future, you must first understand your current financial position. Assess your assets, liabilities, and overall financial health. You are required to learn how to create a financial snapshot that serves as the foundation for strategic planning.

Regularly review your financial standing by updating your net worth statement.

List all your assets and liabilities. Update this statement annually to track your progress and adjust your financial strategies accordingly.

8. Retirement Planning:

You may be at the retirement stage. Before reaching there, retirement may seem distant, but early planning is crucial. For your retirement plan delve into retirement planning strategies, set realistic retirement goals, and choose appropriate savings tools. Whether you're just starting your career or approaching retirement age, find guidance on creating a sustainable retirement plan.

Start saving for retirement as early as possible.

Contribute to retirement accounts by getting benefits from these suggestions: educate yourself and encourage financial literacy, create a budget for retirement, diversify investments, assign a part of emergency fund for retirement, regularly review and adjust, and you can check potential retirement plan in the society you live in as a backup plan.

By the end of this chapter, you do not only have a deeper understanding of the foundations of financial health but also possess the practical tools and insights needed to take control of your financial destiny. Embrace the knowledge within these pages, apply the strategies outlined, and embark on a transformative journey toward financial empowerment and a secure future.

As the last takeaway from this chapter, I used to teach my students that good investment is the one that while you're asleep, the investment can protect itself. Implement this in any kinds of investment you hold including investing in yourself and personal development. This a principle in the "Selfcation" lifestyle.

Chapter 17

Career Development and Achieving Success

C areer development is a crucial aspect of personal growth. This chapter guides you through the process of setting and achieving professional goals, advancing in your career, and finding success in the workplace. It explores topics such as goal-setting, networking, skills development, and leadership. By the end of this chapter, you will be better prepared to navigate your career path and achieve your desired level of success. Below are some insights to help you in your career development and achieving success.

1. Setting Professional Goals:

One of the foundational steps in career development is the art of goal-setting. We discussed goal setting in the previous chapters, e.g. chapters 6, 7, and 9, but here specifically we refer to goal setting related to career development. One of the vital points here is the importance of defining clear and achievable objectives. Understanding how to articulate and pursue your professional aspirations is key to crafting a fulfilling and purpose-driven career.

Determine where you want to be in the next five years; you can change the timeframe as per your desire. Set your professional goals to achieve your future position. You need to set goals to turn your future vision into reality. You may refer to your letter to your future self that you wrote in chapter 2 and edit or rewrite the professional and career part. Once you know where you want to be in five years from now, you can design your current roadmap to achieve there.

2. Advancing in Your Career:

Climbing the professional ladder requires strategic planning and execution. You need to explore actionable strategies for advancing in your career, whether it involves seeking promotions, transitioning to new roles, or excelling in your current position.

Seek to enhance your professional skills to stay updated. Additionally, explore related skills to broaden your expertise. You have two options: specialise in one field and devote yourself to it, or become proficient in a few fields to have a backup. The decision is yours. Just a quick reminder that don't put all your eggs in one basket.

3. Exploring Topics Like Networking:

Building and nurturing professional connections is a skill that can significantly impact your career trajectory. Discover sources to cultivate meaningful relationships that can open doors to new opportunities and enhance your professional reputation.

Thanks to technology, now we have the opportunity of virtual networking. Beware of the usage of social media to support your career development. Be specific in your virtual presence.

4. Skills Development for Success:

Continuous learning and skills development are essential components of a thriving career. Continuing Professional Development (CPD) courses can serve as valuable resources to guide you in this regard. It is crucial to identify and acquire the necessary skills and knowledge to stay competent in your field. From technical skills to soft skills, equipping yourself with the tools for ongoing professional growth is vital in your journey of "Selfcation". Life-long learning is a factor that you need add to your "Selfcation" lifestyle.

5. Leadership Principles:

Whether you're aiming for a leadership role or seeking to enhance your leadership capabilities, understanding the principles of effective leadership is crucial. Explore leadership concepts, learn how to inspire and guide others, and discover the traits that set successful leaders apart.

Leadership principles are fundamental guidelines and beliefs that inform the actions and decisions of effective leaders. These principles provide a framework for leading individuals or teams toward shared goals and fostering a positive and productive work environment. While leadership principles can vary, here are some commonly recognised ones that you can practice them and benefit from:

Lead by Example: Effective leaders set the standard for others by demonstrating the behaviour and work ethic they expect from their team Leading by example builds trust and credibility.

Communicate Clearly: Clear and transparent communication is essential for effective leadership. Leaders must articulate their vision, and expectations, and provide timely feedback to ensure everyone is on the same page.

Inspire and Motivate: Leaders should inspire and motivate their team members to achieve their best potential. This involves recognising and celebrating achievements, providing encouragement, and nurturing a positive work environment.

Empower and Delegate: Effective leaders empower their team members by delegating tasks and responsibilities. Trusting others with important assignments not only develops their skills but also creates a sense of ownership and responsibility. Having a sense of belonging can add value. The sense of belonging is often associated with improved well-being, increased motivation, and enhanced productivity, among other positive outcomes.

Decisiveness: Leaders must make informed and timely decisions. Indecisiveness can lead to confusion and inefficiency. Decisive leaders assess information quickly and take appropriate action.

Adaptability: The ability to adapt to changing circumstances and embrace innovation is crucial for effective leadership. Leaders who can navigate change inspire confidence in their team.

Integrity and Ethics: Leaders should uphold high standards of integrity and ethical behaviour. Trust is the foundation of effective leadership, and maintaining honesty and ethical conduct is essential.

Accountability: Leaders take responsibility for their actions and the outcomes of their decisions. They also hold their team members accountable for their responsibilities and commitments.

Continuous Learning: Effective leaders are committed to their own personal and professional development. They seek out opportunities to learn and grow, staying updated in their industry and enhancing their leadership skills.

Cultivate a Positive Culture: Leaders play a key role in shaping the organisational culture. Fostering a positive, inclusive, and collaborative culture contributes to the overall success and satisfaction of the team.

Build Relationships: Effective leaders prioritise building strong relationships with team members, colleagues, and stakeholders. Building rapport and understanding individual strengths and weaknesses is crucial for a cohesive team.

Resilience: Leaders need to demonstrate resilience in the face of challenges and setbacks. Remaining optimistic during difficult times helps maintain team morale.

These principles serve as a foundation for effective leadership and can be adapted to different contexts and industries. Leadership is dynamic, and successful leaders often integrate these principles into their unique leadership styles while remaining flexible to meet the needs of their teams and organisations.

Here is the only section where intentionally I used 'they' instead of 'you'. I wanted to highlight the charisma and charm of a leader, encouraging the recognition of these qualities to incorporate the principles into your life and strive to become an exemplary leader in your "Selfcation" journey. Please note that if you cannot lead your life, others will do it for you. In the "Selfcation" journey you need to sit in the driver's seat and lead your life.

6.   Your Path to Success:

Pay attention and remind yourself that you are on the path to success no matter what is going on during your journey. As you progress, you will gain valuable insights and practical strategies to be better prepared to navigate your career path with confidence, armed with the knowledge and skills needed to achieve your desired level of success in the professional world. Observe the path as well as your endeavour through the path of "Selfcation" and reflect to yourself.

To sum up, this chapter is a roadmap for your professional development empowering you to proactively shape your career, set meaningful goals, build a robust professional network, continually enhance your skills and knowledge and embrace the principles of effective leadership. In the coming chapter taking the "Selfcation" approach to finance and career development will be explained in more detail.

Thumbs up. You nailed it. Treat yourself to a delicious snack.

Visualise yourself in the desired financial and professional aspects of your life and then, move on to the next chapter.

Chapter 18

Taking the "Selfcation" Approach to Finances and Career Development

Y ou will discover how applying a "Selfcation" mindset can positively impact your financial and career decisions. This approach emphasises aligning financial and professional goals with personal values and aspirations. This chapter explores how aligning financial decisions and career choices with personal values and aspirations can lead to greater life satisfaction. You need to make financial and career decisions that resonate with your authentic self, allowing you to create a more rewarding and satisfying life in your "Selfcation" journey. Finance and career development in the "Selfcation" mindset, can be achieved through the following practices. Do you have your notebook and pen with you?

1. Values Alignment Exercise:

Create a list of your top five values.

Connect your values to specific financial and career decisions. Assess how well your current choices align with these values.

2. Career Vision Board:

Develop a vision board for your career.

Visualise and articulate your ideal professional path. Incorporate elements that represent your authentic self and career aspirations. You've just visualised the desired version of yourself in financial and professional aspects. Get help from it to tailor your best version in your "Selfcation" journey.

3. Self-Reflection Assignment:

Take dedicated time for self-reflection.

Reflect on the previous practices, i.e., values and vision.

4. Financial Life Audit:

Conduct an audit of your current financial situation.

Evaluate your financial decisions against your values. Identify areas where adjustments can be made to align with your authentic self.

5. Networking with Purpose:

Engage in purposeful networking.

Connect with professionals who share your values and align with your career goals. Explore collaborations and opportunities that resonate with your authentic self.

6. Skill Enhancement Plan:

Develop a plan for enhancing your skills.

Identify skills that align with your career aspirations and values. Create a roadmap for acquiring or improving these skills. Also, create a measure to navigate your progress.

7. Financial Goal Setting:

Set clear financial goals for the short and long term.

Align your financial objectives with your authentic self. Define milestones that reflect your values and contribute to your overall well-being.

8. Mentorship Exploration:

Explore mentorship opportunities.

Seek mentors who resonate with your values and career path. Learn from their experiences and insights to add value to your "Selfcation" journey.

9. Reflective Journaling:

Maintain a reflective journal throughout the process.

Document your thoughts, insights, and challenges. Regular reflection will help track your progress and reinforce your commitment to "Selfcation".

10. Integrating Action Plan:

Develop an action plan for integrating with other aspects of your "Selfcation" journey.

Create a step-by-step plan for incorporating the principles of "Selfcation" into your daily financial and professional decision-making.

This suggested "Selfcation" practices and roadmap provides a structured approach to exploring and integrating the "Selfcation" mindset into various aspects of your life, nurturing a journey toward a more authentic, fulfilling, and purpose-driven existence.

Up to this point, we have explored understanding the "Selfcation" journey and its implementation. You implemented the suggestion step by step. Now, it's time to explore how to embrace change and transformation. You've been living with your previous mindset and lifestyle, and in one word, previous you for a long time. Be patient in your development journey. You are on the right track to unleash your potential. You need to be prepared fully to handle and manage your potential before it comes to realisation. Educate yourself and learn how to fully accept your new "Selfcation" version.

Vision without action is merely a dream. Action without vision just passes the time. Vision with action can change the world.

Joel A. Barker

8. Embracing Change and Transformation:

E mbracing Change and Transformation refers to the willingness and ability to welcome and adapt to new circumstances, ideas, or perspectives in your "Selfcation" journey. It involves a proactive and positive approach to transitions and shifts, recognising them as opportunities for growth, improvement, and personal development. In the coming chapters adapting to change and uncertainty, embracing transformation and personal evolution, and finally reinventing yourself in the "Selfcation" way will be explained.

Chapter 19

Adapting to Change and Uncertainty

Change and uncertainty are inevitable and constant aspects of human existence. This chapter equips you with skills to navigate and deal with them successfully. You will explore the importance of adaptability and resilience when facing change and uncertainty. Practical strategies, coping mechanisms, and exercises will help you embrace change as an opportunity for growth rather than a source of stress and threat.

When we talk about uncertainty, there is a common pitfall that uncertainty and risk are considered the same. Before we start off this chapter, we should keep in mind the difference between these two.

In a situation of uncertainty, not all consequences of a given action or decision can be known. It is different from a situation of risk. In a situation of risk, it is possible to know all the possible outcomes of a certain action.

The concept of risk is amenable to probability calculus, offering a robust foundation for risk management, cost/benefit analysis, budget planning, and related activities. Probability calculations provide a structured approach to assessing the likelihood of different outcomes.

In situations of uncertainty, the probability calculus has no sound foundation. Unlike in scenarios involving risk, where probabilities can be assigned to potential outcomes, uncertainty implies a lack of clear, measurable probabilities. In such cases, there is no objective basis for traditional risk management, cost/benefit analysis, and other control techniques that rely on precise probability assessments. In real life, for almost all decisions going beyond routine, uncertainty exists. Navigating uncertainty requires a more adaptive and qualitative approach, often involving scenario planning, resilience-building strategies, and flexible decision-making.

Adapting to change and uncertainty involves cultivating a mindset and adopting strategies that enable you to trace and thrive in dynamic and unpredictable environments. Here are key principles for adapting to change and uncertainty:

1. Cultivate Flexibility:

Embrace flexibility in thinking and action. Be open to different perspectives and adaptable to shifting circumstances. The flexible "Selfcation" mindset allows for creative problem-solving and quick adjustments. Openness to experience is one of the personality characteristics as per the Five Factor Model of Personality in case you want to know more about this trait.

2. Continuous Learning:

Nurture a culture of continuous learning. Stay curious, seek new knowledge, and acquire skills that enhance your ability to adapt to evolving situations. Embrace the growth mindset of "Selfcation" that sees challenges as opportunities for learning. Also, they can assist you to stretch your safe zone.

3. Resilience Building:

Develop resilience to bounce back from setbacks. Resilient view challenges as temporary and learn from adversity. Building emotional resilience helps you to manage stress during uncertain times. Emotion regulation in DBT can be implemented here as well.

4. Agile Decision-Making:

Adopt agile decision-making processes. Break down complex problems into manageable steps and be prepared to adjust course based on feedback and new information. Iterate quickly to respond to changing circumstances. While maintaining a long-term goal, remain open to adjusting your plan based on observations and reflections regarding your current actions. Understand that adaptation may require patience, and some changes might take time to yield positive results. Avoid reactive, short-term thinking. Withhold impulsive reaction by techniques such as STOP that is used in DBT. It is acronym of Stop, Take a step back, Observe, and Proceed mindfully.

5. Scenario Planning:

Engage in scenario planning to anticipate possible futures. Identify different scenarios and develop strategies for each. This allows for more informed actions like decision-making when uncertainties unfold. Consider your abilities as well as inabilities. This knowledge helps you in better planning for scenarios.

6. Collaboration and Networking:

Improve collaboration and build strong networks. Working with others enhances problem-solving capabilities and provides support during challenging times. Collaboration also brings diverse perspectives to the table.

7. Embrace Innovation:

Encourage a culture of innovation. Explore new ideas, technologies, and approaches. Innovation is often a response to change and can lead to improved processes and outcomes. Sometimes you can optimise your sources and your energy distribution in a better way by being innovative.

8. Focus on What You Can Control:

Concentrate on aspects within your control. While uncertainties may exist, identify and focus on factors you can influence allows for a sense of agency and empowerment. Some of the events you cannot control are facts that you need to accept and adjust your lifestyle to reduce the disturbance and unnecessary discomfort in your life.

9. Self-Care:

Prioritise self-care to maintain well-being. A healthy mindset and physical well-being contribute to better coping mechanisms and strategies during times of change and uncertainty. In chapter 13 we talked about self-care in detail. The point worth mentioning here is in uncertain situations, stress level is high. From neurological perspective Pre-Frontal Cortetx (PFC) of our brain is responsible for cognitive abilities and executive functions is impacted negatively due to stress. Self-care can help PFC function in uncertain situations.

10. Feedback Loops:

Establish feedback loops to continuously assess and adjust strategies. Regular feedback and monitoring are key indicators provide valuable insights for adaptation. Make sure you don't get trapped in the loop of developing obsession. Obsession involves the urge to conduct the same rituals without results. Be careful not to get stuck in this trap.

Adapting to change and uncertainty is an ongoing process that requires a combination of mindset, skills, and strategic approaches in the "Selfcation" journey. By cultivating resilience, embracing flexibility, and fostering a culture of continuous learning, you can navigate uncertain environments with greater effectiveness and resilience and step by step you get closer to welcoming the "Selfcation" lifestyle. In the next chapter, we talk about embracing transformation and personal evolution.

Chapter 20

Embracing Transformation and Personal Evolution

ersonal growth often involves transformation and evolution. You will explore the significance of continuous growth and how to embrace personal transformation in your "Selfcation" journey. Also, this chapter again explores the significance of lifelong learning, self-improvement, and the evolving self. Practical advice and examples will inspire you to continue evolving and growing throughout your life. Moreover, you will learn to embrace these processes as constructive and transformative experiences.

1. Continuous Growth:

Understanding personal growth as an ongoing process is fundamental. Discover the significance of consistently challenging yourself, setting new goals, and adapting to change as key elements in the journey of self-discovery in the "Selfcation" path. Accepting uncertainty is the only certain thing in life, is a leap forward. Get along with life's uncertainty and change your perspective. Uncertainty brings the opportunity for improvement.

2. Lifelong Learning and Self-Improvement:

Explore the transformative power of lifelong learning and self-improvement. Every experience, whether successful or challenging, contributes to your personal growth. Learn how to cultivate a mindset of curiosity and adaptability that fuels a lifetime of learning.

As soon as you feel comfortable in your life-long learning goal, come up with another plan for your ongoing learning in the "Selfcation" journey. You need to feel comfortable in challenging yourself.

In the process of transformation and development, you experience life and death. Death of previous self and life of the new self. Seize this experience to welcome new you in the "Selfcation" journey and observe your progress and improvement.

3. The Evolving Self:

Recognise and appreciate the evolving nature of the self. As you progress through different stages of life, your values, perspectives, and aspirations may evolve. You need to navigate these changes and understand them as integral parts of your personal growth in the "Selfcation" journey.

4. Practical Suggestions and Examples:

Practical suggestions and real-life examples will inspire and guide you. Discover actionable steps and learn from the experiences of others who have embraced personal growth. Read biographies. These life stories convey tangible insights that can assist you in applying the principles of "Selfcation" to your unique journey.

We talked about role model in chapter 3 and 4. You can refer to those chapters to refresh your mind on this. A role model is just an example. You may refer to those you admire, but not consider them your role model. Those you admire can be source of inspiration.

5. Positive and Transformative Experiences:

Shift your perspective on personal growth and transformation. Reframe these processes as positive and transformative experiences rather than destruction. By embracing change and continuous evolution, you'll learn to navigate the complexities of personal development with resilience and enthusiasm in the "Selfcation" journey.

In summary, this chapter is your guide to embrace the transformative potential of your personal growth. Whether through continuous learning, self-improvement, or understanding the evolving nature of the self, you gain practical insights and inspiration to cultivate a mindset of lifelong growth. Embrace the journey of becoming the most authentic and satisfied version of yourself through positive and transformative experiences. You need to recognise this process of change and transformation as a journey from being to becoming. 'Becoming' conveys the message of transformation and development that you've aspired for. Now we move on to the next chapter to reinvent yourself in your "Selfcation" journey.

Chapter 21

Reinventing Yourself in Your "Selfcation" Journey

E xcellent work. You are here in the last chapter to reinvent yourself in your "Selfcation" journey. The final chapter encourages you to apply the principles of the "Selfcation" mindset in your ongoing journey of reinvention of yourself and self-improvement. Sometimes, reinvention is the key to personal growth, accomplishment, and gratification. It explores the principles of reinvention, strategies for self-reinvention, and the benefits of aligning this process with personal values and aspirations. Recognise reinvention is the key to unlocking new dimensions of personal growth and fulfillment. Following are suggestions to assist you in reinventing yourself in your "Selfcation" journey. Are you all set? Let's kick off the last chapter.

1.   Principles of Reinvention:

Explore the foundational principles that underpin the process of reinvention. Understand how embracing change and aligning your actions with your authentic self can lead to profound transformations in various aspects of your life.

Among the principles of reinvention is the courage to change. Embrace change with courage. In chapter 12 you read 'Don't consider vulnerability and courage as poles apart; they can be seen as two sides of the same coin'. Think about the flow of courage and vulnerability. Tune into it.

Self-reinvention often requires stepping out of your comfort zone, confronting fears, and taking risks. By being willing to challenge old habits and beliefs, remaining open to new experiences and learning, cultivating resilience in the face of setbacks, and building self-empowerment, you can reinvent yourself.

Create a personal manifesto outlining the principles that will guide your process of reinvention. Refer to chapter 12. Reflect on values such as authenticity, adaptability, and continuous growth. Regularly revisit and refine this manifesto as you progress on your journey.

Understanding these principles helps you navigate the complexities of personal transformation. It provides a framework for making decisions and taking actions aligned with the goals of reinvention in your "Selfcation" journey.

Now in reinventing yourself take a huge step forward and come up with a personal motto that echoes yourself with the minimum number of words. Take an example from the current book name. "Selfcation" can convey the message the whole book is presenting. Come up with a motto that can be your mantra.

2. Strategies for Self-Reinvention:

Explore effective strategies for self-reinvention. Follow the insights and strategies you have learned so far to take practical and actionable steps to guide you through the process of redefining and reshaping your identity, aspirations, and goals. Observe and navigate challenges and leverage opportunities for meaningful reinvention.

Develop a detailed action plan for your self-reinvention. Identify specific goals, skills to acquire, and steps to take. Break down the plan into manageable tasks and set deadlines. Regularly assess your progress and adjust the plan as needed. Keep this action plan as a measure for your improvement and you can revisit and edit it from time to time. Self-monitoring is the key to the whole process of the "Selfcation".

3. Benefits of Alignment with Personal Values:

Understand the transformative impact of aligning the process of reinvention with your values and aspirations. Discover how this alignment can lead to a more authentic and satisfying life. Explore the symbiotic relationship between your values and the continual process of self-improvement and ensure that the process of reinvention is in harmony with your values and aspirations.

Conduct a value assessment to identify your core beliefs and aspirations. Evaluate your current goals and actions to ensure alignment with these values. Make adjustments where necessary and reflect on how this alignment contributes to a more fulfilling journey.

Aligning reinvention with personal values adds depth and authenticity to the process. It ensures that the changes made are not only transformative superficially but also resonate with your core beliefs, leading to a more fulfilling outcome in your "Selfcation" journey.

4. Encouragement for Ongoing Journey:

This component signifies motivation and support for the ongoing journey of self-improvement and reinvention. It acknowledges that personal growth is a continual process rather than a destination. You can refer to chapter 9 to refresh your mind on staying motivated and focused.

Don't forget to keep a journal where you regularly document your successes, challenges, and reflections on your "Selfcation" journey. Use this journal as a source of encouragement, noting how far you've come and identify areas for further growth.

Share your reflections with a mentor or support group for added encouragement. By encouraging, you inspire yourself to view your journey as a dynamic and evolving process. It reinforces the idea that embracing change is not a one-time event but an ongoing exploration that calls for your curiosity and enthusiasm. You need to keep the fire inside you burning to push yourself forward. Keep the fire burning and enjoy its warmth, but don't let it turn everything to ashes. You need to be alert in your "Selfcation" journey.

5. Dynamic Nature of "Selfcation":

"Selfcation" is portrayed as dynamic, indicating that its principles evolve in tandem with personal growth and development. During this process you challenge yourself, question yourself, and revisit yourself very often to improve yourself in the "Selfcated" journey.

Write a reflective text or create a visual representation that captures the evolution of your understanding of authenticity. Highlight specific moments or experiences that have influenced your perception. Include your future self in it as well. Share this reflection with a trusted friend or mentor to gain additional perspectives.

Recognising the dynamic nature emphasises that the principles are adaptable and responsive to your progress. It encourages you to embrace change and continually refine your understanding of authenticity regardless of uncertainties that exist in life.

6. Emphasis on Change as an Opportunity:

Validate change as an opportunity for continual self-improvement rather than a challenge. Identify a recent challenge or change in your life. Write a reflection on how you approached it as an opportunity for growth rather than a setback. Explore the positive outcomes and lessons learned. Share your insights with a peer or mentor.

This reframes the mindset around change, nurturing the "Selfcation" mindset. It encourages you to approach challenges as opportunities for growth, making the journey of reinvention of yourself more empowering and fruitful for a new you to be born in your "Selfcation" journey.

In summary, the final chapter integrates principles, strategies, and encouragement to guide you in your ongoing journey of reinvention and self-improvement. It serves as a signpost for your ongoing journey. It reinforces the idea that the principles of the "Selfcation" are not static; they evolve as you evolve.

The encouragement to embrace reinvention emphasises the dynamic nature of personal growth and encourages you to view change as an opportunity for continual self-improvement. As you apply these principles, you find resilience, authenticity, and satisfaction in your unique journey of becoming the most authentic version of yourself in your "Selfcation" journey. The person resembles nobody, but yourself. You are unique. Reinventing yourself is a deliberate intervention you do.

Finally, you become "SELFCATED" and the best version of yourself so far. Still there is a way for improvement. You got the hang of being on personal development path in your "Selfcation" journey. You nailed it. High five.

The illiterate of the 21st century will not be those who cannot read and write, but those who cannot learn, unlearn, and relearn.

Alvin Toffler

Conclusion:

Hope you enjoyed your journey of "Selfcation". It was a pleasure to accompany you during this exploration. In the last part of the book, we will reflect on your "Selfcation" journey and then chart the path forward with a "Selfcation" mindset.

In the process of "Selfcation", you discover many things about yourself and you recognise your strengths and identify areas that need more attention for improvement. You lay off destructive layers that were added to you in your life. Now in the "Selfcation" journey, you are creating and reinventing yourself, the new you.

Reflecting on Your "Selfcation" Journey

You need to reflect on your "Selfcation" journey and the progress you've made. Embarking on the comprehensive journey through these 21 chapters has been a rich exploration into the multifaceted aspects of personal development. Each chapter, a stepping stone in this transformative expedition, has provided valuable insights, practical strategies, and profound reflections.

From laying the foundational principles of "Selfcation" to delving into specific realms like financial well-being, career development, and personal growth, the journey has been a holistic exploration. The emphasis on self-reflection continuous learning, and resilience has threaded its way through various topics, highlighting their universal importance in the pursuit of authenticity and satisfaction.

The call to "Selfcation" extends beyond a mere concept; it is an invitation to actively shape your life in alignment with personal values and aspirations. The assignments proposed in each chapter, designed to be practical and introspective, serve as guiding lights in applying the principles discussed.

As we conclude this transformative expedition, may these insights and practical steps resonate with you, guide you on your unique life path to "Selfcation". Embrace change with courage, recognise vulnerability, celebrate the journey's triumphs and challenges, and acknowledge that the quest for authenticity is not a destination but a lifelong adventure.

May the principles shared throughout these chapters serve as compass points, steering towards a more authentic, fulfilling existence. In the ongoing journey of "Selfcation", let the knowledge gained here be a source of empowerment, resilience, and inspiration, propelling you towards the most authentic version of yourself.

Don't wait for anybody to save you. You are responsible for your life and you need to take initiative for your growth to be a better version of yourself. The only person you cannot escape from is you. You need to consider yourself as the number one priority of your life. It is not selfish, it is the "Selfcation". You need to entitle yourself first and then others will recognise you in the same manner.

It is beneficial to write a code of conduct for yourself to be accountable in your "Selfcation" journey. Revisit this code of conduct from time to time to do any potential adjustments as well as alterations.

Charting the Path Forward with a "Selfcation" Mindset

To wrap up the book, it is inviting you to reflect on your journey. It encourages you to celebrate your progress and empowers you to continue your path of personal development and self-improvement. You are inspired to chart your future with a "Selfcation" mindset, carrying with you the empowerment you've gained throughout the book to reach your desired future you.

You are equipped with a toolbox that contains insights and practical strategies for embracing change, transforming yourself, and reinventing yourself in alignment with your authentic self. Now, you are well prepared to accept, adapt to change, embrace personal growth, and navigate life's transformations by believing and trusting yourself.

Pull up your socks and go back to your life's battles. This time, fight better because you are more determined, armed, and equipped for the challenges of life.

You nailed it and now you are **SELFCATED**.

Made in the USA
Columbia, SC
26 June 2024

37442859R00083